The Way of Faith

The Way of Faith

words of admonition and encouragement for the journey based on The Letter to the Hebrews

James M. Pitts, Editor

CHANTICLEER PUBLISHING COMPANY, INC.
Wake Forest, North Carolina

THE WAY OF FAITH

International Standard Book Number 0-913029-10-6

Front Cover Illustration:
a view of Jerusalem from the Franciscan Dominus Flevit Chapel ("The Lord Wept") on the Mount of Olives. The name of the chapel is a reminder that when Jesus came to Jerusalem for the last time, he wept over the city (Luke 19:41). Photograph by James M. Pitts.

CHANTICLEER PUBLISHING COMPANY, INC.
P. O. Box 501
Wake Forest, North Carolina 27587

Contents

Special Thanks

are extended to my colleagues in chaplaincy at Furman University, Dr. Victor A. Greene, Jr. and Mrs. Shirley Smith. Their partnership in solicited advice and proofreading encouraged the successful completion of this endeavor.

Also, I am thankful to my many teachers, most of whom are students, who have taught me much through our shared learning and serving experiences in our journey toward maturity.

James M. Pitts

Preface

This collection of sermons, articles and commentaries represents both commonality and diversity. Each deals with the New Testament writing titled "To the Hebrews." Each is authored by a contemporary person recognized as a competent scholar or capable minister. All are Baptists and share a common faith confession believing "Jesus is Lord!"

Their approaches to Scripture, styles of communication, and assessments of themes represent a delightful diversity. As editor, I have attempted to celebrate the pluralism of the Baptist fellowship. Therefore, this is not a uniform lesson series, but intentionally an uneven collage by a variety of contributors.

They were chosen because they are either colleagues, friends or acquaintances. A number have participated as faculty for the Furman University Pastors School held each summer during the week of July 4th.

In reviewing the list of contributors, you will see that some are "household names" in the Baptist family. They are firmly established in their careers and respected for lives of dedicated service. Others are well on their way toward professional maturity. A few are now at the beginning of their career journey and already evidence great promise. Representing all ages, male and female, black and white, they are a rich sampler of our "unity in diversity."

Fortunately, they responded positively to my request for their contribution. As you read and consider their work, I trust you will come to see them all as lovers of God, servants of Christ, and students of Scripture.

No attempt has been made by the editor or publisher to direct the individual contributors, other than suggesting a specific portion of the biblical text. As is the custom in the free church tradition, no imprimatur for orthodoxy has been sought in Dallas, Atlanta, Nashville, or Rome.

I express my enthusiastic appreciation to these contributors, who took time from other responsibilities to complete their assignment. Also, I have been honored by their willingness to trust me to present their views as they chose to express them. I thank Chanticleer Publishing Company of Wake Forest, North Carolina for the privilege of convening these authors and collating their manuscripts.

I hope that this publication will encourage similar endeavors demonstrating, both within and outside the Baptist fellowship, the richness of our shared faith and priceless heritage of religious liberty and freedom of expression. In community and conversation, may we continue to listen and learn, encouraging one another in our faith pilgrimage toward Christian maturity.

James M. Pitts
Furman University
April 20, 1985

1

An Introduction to Hebrews

Edgar V. McKnight
William R. Kenan, Jr. Professor of Religion
Furman University, Greenville, South Carolina

I. The Conventional Historical-Critical Approach

An introduction to a biblical book is normally a discussion of what is known about the historical origins of the book. Such an introduction for Hebrews is easy: we do not know who wrote Hebrews; we do not know to whom it was written; we do not know precisely why it was written; we do not even know how to classify the book as a writing. Hebrews is indeed the "riddle" of the New Testament.

The effort to situate Hebrews historically and to make sense of the content in light of that historical situation is a result of the historical-critical heritage. In its application to the Bible as a whole, this approach has been very valuable. The historical-critical approach corrected and/or deepened religious and theological insights which had developed with the earlier dogmatic approach. Helmut Koester of Harvard University, however, has suggested that the enterprise of historical New Testament introduction

> . . . has never managed to become an enterprise which is central for the vital interests of religious, theological and historical understanding. At best, it has been useful as an ancillary discipline, helping to secure genuine source-materials for scho-

> lars who wanted to base their discussions on reliable information; or aiding theologians who wanted to affirm the authenticity of canonical writings on which they based their doctrines and dogmas.[1]

If information concerning the historical origins of biblical books is ancillary for theological and religious study of New Testament writings in general, how much more subordinate is it for appreciation of Hebrews! Robert Jewett has lamented the fact that the dilemmas of Hebrews make it difficult to gain "an overview or even a sense of what the argument is all about." Although Hebrews "contains many eloquent texts for sermonizing, its argument as a whole, has never played a decisive role for the Christian Community."[2]

Solutions to the problem of understanding Hebrews today are usually sought within the historical-critical paradigm. Most commentators suggest a specific historical and religious situation which may be seen as the problem or the "question" to which Hebrews is the "answer." Then commentators admit the tentativeness of their reconstruction and offer an exegesis which is not directly and necessarily coordinated with the introductory information. Hugh Montefiore, for example, argues that Hebrews was written by Apollos to the Church of Corinth, especially to the Jewish Christians in that congregation. In Montefiore's opinion, it was written from Ephesus in A. D. 52-54, prior to First Corinthians. The commentary, however, "has been constructed in the hope that it may be of use to those for whom there is as yet no convincing solution to the difficult problems which this Epistle poses."[3]

Jewett feels that effective exegesis of Hebrews demands specificity which is gained when a particular hypothesis concerning the writer's situation is selected and used in interpre-

1. Helmut Koester, "New Testament Introduction: A Critique of a Discipline," p. 6. Koester, however, has suggested that the discipline be reformed so that it may become relevant to contemporary religious, theological and historical understanding. He would advocate a rigorous historical approach and not the more literary approach which I advocate.

2. Robert Jewett, *Letter to Pilgrims: A Commentary on the Epistle to the Hebrews*, pp. 2-3.

3. Hugh Montefiore, *The Epistle to the Hebrews*, p. 32.

tation. "If one were to select an audience hypothesis that seems most plausible and then take the imaginative leap of perceiving each verse as directly related to that situation, the fire of the argument might ignite and the sparks could easily leap across time to the modern situation."[4] Jewett suggests that Hebrews be read as a letter of Epaphras to the churches of the Lycus Valley designed to combat a unique Jewish-Gnostic heresy (evidenced in Colossians). It would have been written at approximately the same time as Colossians to deal with the same sort of situation.

The suggestion of Helmut Koester that the writing be appreciated not in light of any specific situation but as a "fundamental theological treatise" seems to move away from the historical paradigm. The nature of the writing as a theological treatise, in the opinion of Koester, is the reason why "every attempt to fix the epistle as a whole in a specific situation of the church or a church group fails.[5] Instead of moving outside the historical-critical argumentation, however, Koester simply generalizes the historical moment which is used for situating and interpreting the writing. In his historical introduction, Koester places Hebrews in the "general situation of the churches after Paul's time." Hebrews, then, is interpreted as "a witness for the efforts to develop the Pauline legacy" during the last decades of the first century.[6]

In the reader-oriented literary introduction which follows in the next section, emphasis is placed upon the potentiality for meaning which the linguistic and literary materials of Hebrews offer. Hebrews makes sense apart from a particular historical setting. Nevertheless, historical data and speculation do set some constraints and can be coordinated with linguistic and literary data to provide meaning and significance for the contemporary reader. Therefore, the basic introductory data will be summarized.

The author. Hebrews is anonymous. In an early period, Hebrews was interpreted as a letter of Paul which was original-

4. Jewett, pp. 3-4.
5. Helmut Koester, " '*Outside the Camp*': Hebrews 13:9-14," p. 315, n. 54.
6. Helmut Koester, *Introduction to the New Testament*, II, p. 272.

ly written in Hebrew or Aramaic and which was translated by Luke into Greek. Other early traditions name Clement of Rome, Apollos, or Barnabas as the author. The vocabulary, style, and argumentation of Hebrews lead modern scholars to discount Pauline authorship and to envision a rhetorically trained and Hellenistically oriented Christian as the author. Modern critics have suggested as author the names of: Stephen, Philip, Peter, Silas, Aristion, Prisca, and Jude.

The recipients. Readers have been sought among Jewish Christians because of the use of the Old Testament and the arguments of the superiority of Jesus and the new covenant to Moses and the old covenant. The original readers were regarded for a long time as Jewish Christians living in Palestine, or more specifically in Jerusalem. Since the discovery of the Dead Sea Scrolls, some scholars have defended the thesis that readers were former members of the Qumran Community — either priests who had been converted to Christianity or former members of the community who had come close to becoming Christians but who had not come all the way.

Some scholars have seen the readers as Jewish Christians outside Palestine — either Jewish Christians spread over the Roman world or Jewish Christians in a particular community (wealthy and cultured Jews at Ephesus, a small conservative enclave of Jewish Christians in Rome, or Jewish Christians in Alexanderia or Cyprus who were being induced to espouse nationalistic Judaism).

The fact that the Old Testament was the Bible for the Christian community everywhere — for Gentile Christians as well as Jewish Christians — makes it impossible to limit the readers to Jewish Christians in or outside of Palestine. The readers, then, may be seen as predominately Gentile Christians or simply Christians in general who are being warned concerning a general lassitude. These Christians have been located in such places as Corinth, Ephesus, the Lycus Valley, Antioch, Rome, or some other Italian community.

The one bit of information in the book itself which may be related to destination is the statement in 13:24 "those from Italy greet you." It is possible that this is simply a greeting from Italy (perhaps Rome), but it is possible that the author is writing to Rome (or elsewhere in Italy) and sending greetings from Italians who are in his vicinity.

The date. Since Clement of Rome refers to Hebrews, the writing had to be in existence before the end of the first century. The use made of the Temple in Hebrews (and silence concerning the destruction of the Temple in 70) constitute no justification for dating the writing before 70 because abstract ideas and not the specific Herodian Temple is at issue.

II. A Reader-Oriented Literary Introduction to Hebrews

This essay introduces a group of sermons on texts from Hebrews. Readers of these sermons are concerned with meaning and significance of Hebrews which goes beyond historically constrained information and meaning. Instead of postulating some particular historical situation which can make Hebrews understandable, Hebrews may be approached by such readers in something of the same way that a literary work is approached. (This approach is particularly well suited for Hebrews, but it is applicable even for books which may be situated more securely in history.)

In following a "literary" rather than a "historical" approach, Aristotle's distinction between literature and history may be a helpful starting point:

> . . . it is not the poet's business to relate actual events, but such things as might or could happen in accordance with probability or necessity. A poet differs from a historian, not because one writes verse and the other prose . . . , but because the historian relates what happened, the poet what might happen. That is why poetry is more akin to philosophy and is a better thing than history; poetry deals with general truths, history with specific events.[7]

To read Hebrews as history is to read it as a specific event, as the result of what happened to particular individuals in a

7. Aristotle, *Poetics*, Ch. 9.

geographically and temporally limited context. To read Hebrews as literature is to read it as universal truth.

Is there a universal motif in Hebrews? Is the failure of the ancient generation of God's people to enter God's rest a warning which transcends place and time? If the book of Hebrews can be situated in the multiplicity of particular historical contexts theorized by scholars, there must be meaning which transcends any one particular situation. This meaning touches Jewish Christians and Gentile Christians, it reaches not only Christians in Palestine but throughout the Graeco-Roman world. This meaning is no more limited temporally than it is geographically. Christians in general, today and yesterday, face the temptation to inattention, disobedience, dullness of hearing, sluggishness. We need the encouragement to earnestness "in realizing the full assurance of hope until the end" (6:11).

What about the theological or Christological affirmation as it is related to the encouragement and warning of Hebrews? How is the finality of Jesus Christ relevant to our time? When the *function* of Hebrews' appeal to the finality of Jesus Christ is appreciated, it may be translated appropriately to our day. The fact that Christians have received a word spoken by a Son who "reflects the glory of God and bears the very stamp of his nature, upholding the universe by his word of power" (1:3) and who is high priest "seated at the right hand of the throne of the Majesty in heaven" (8:1) is not to be used to justify a contemporary Christian triumphalism. The message was to encourage a small group of suffering Christians, not to make them persecutors.

The function of Hebrews' Christology leads to the question of the literary genre of the book. When we move to a universal context in order to understand and appreciate the content of Hebrews, we also move to a concern with the genre, language, and literary style. Conventional introductions examine the question of the genre of Hebrews because it does not so easily fit the categories used for other New Testament books (gospel, letter, apocalypse). A reader-oriented literary approach shares this concern with genre, not simply in order to answer an historical question but to enable the contemporary reader to read Hebrews appropriately. What *sort* of writing is Hebrews? How is Hebrews to be read? As a letter? Hebrews lacks the distinctive first century salutation. Moreover, through chapter 12 the writing is too impersonal to call it a genuine letter. (The epistolary ending may have been added by a later hand or by the author to give the writing the characteristics of a Pauline letter or to accompany the sermon when it was sent to yet another community.) Is Hebrews a theological treatise? We usually think of a theological treatise as being less practically oriented than Hebrews. A sermon? The writing describes itself as a "word of exhortation" (13:22), and we might begin by thinking of it as a sermon. But it is a particular type sermon, one which is based on Old Testament Scripture interpreted in a fashion reminiscent of the Alexandrian Judaism represented by Philo.

Hebrews and the other books of the New Testament looked at Old Testament writings not in the context of the original situations or even in the context of the Old Testament community as a whole. What was sought was not an original dated message to ancient communities. The Old Testament writings were examined in the context of the church to discern the message to the contemporary community. The Old Testament was examined in light of Jesus with the conviction that Jesus opens up the true meaning of the Old Testament.

Particular methods are used in Hebrews to allow Old Testament passages to speak to the present: the present is seen as the time of fulfillment of Old Testament promises; specific Old Testament persons, events, or things are seen as types which are related to their counterparts in the age of fulfillment; and Old Testament passages are seen as allegories which refer to the period of fulfillment. In one respect, Hebrews is rather unique among New Testament books — the assumption and use of a Platonic world view which sees the visible world of phenomena as an exteriorization, an imperfect imitation of the intelligible world. Material and sensible objects are not ultimate; more ultimate and "real" are the archetypes laid up in heaven. (The Platonic idealism of Hebrews is so pronounced that some scholars have attempted to defend the thesis that the author of Hebrews had a direct acquaintance with Philo and his attempt to reconcile Greek logic with Old Testament teachings.)

Hebrews emphasizes that only the invisible, heavenly, future things constitute reality. A challenging task is to translate the author's meaning from ancient concepts into concepts which are relevant to the reader's world. The use of the idea of the earthly sanctuary as a copy of the heavenly dwelling place of God, for example, is used to stress that "in the heavenly and eternal sanctuary where Christ ministers, His people inevitably enjoy more direct and permanent access to God through Him than would be possible in any earthly and material shrine."[8] How are we to envision the heavenly and eternal sanctuary in our day? F. F. Bruce says:

> We must not think that because our author speaks of Jesus as having "passed through the heavens" and having "sat down at the right hand of the throne of God" he thought of the heavenly sanctuary as being, in reverse, a glorified replica of the sanctuary on earth, established in perpetuity on some higher plane. He uses pictorial language indeed, but uses it to denote realities of a spiritual order, where men and women, inwardly purified from a polluting conscience draw near to God to worship Him in spirit and in truth. This "perfection" is the inauguration of the eschatology which is soon to be consummated. The sanctuary in which they worship God through Christ is the fellowship of the new covenant; it consists in the communion of saints. The house of God, over which Christ, as His Son, is Lord, comprises His people, if we hold fast our boldness and the glorying of our hope" (Ch. 3:6).[9]

It is clear from the concepts into which Bruce translates the concepts of Hebrews that we will find no timeless vocabulary into which to render the message of Hebrews. Whether we use another first century conceptualization (which we have made our own) or more modern concepts, our vocabulary must be faithful to the affective meaning-effect of the language and style of Hebrews as well as to the argumentation on the cognitive level.

8. F. F. Bruce, *The Epistle to the Hebrews*, p. lvii.
9. Bruce, pp. lvii-lviii.

The structure of Hebrews is related to its function as a word of exhortation and to its character as an exposition of Old Testament passages. There is an interweaving of theological argument and earnest exhortation (2:1-4; 3:7-4:11; 4:14-16; 5:11-6:12; 10:19-29; and 12:1-13;17 contain explicit exhortations). In the argument and exhortation the Psalter is used extensively. The usual practice is to quote a section of the Psalter and then to use words and phrases from that quotation in the following exposition. At times the argument is elaborated with use of additional Old Testament passages which deal with the same theme. The exegesis of Psalm 95:7-11 in the exhortation of 3:7-4:13 contains references to the narrative of the wilderness wanderings; and the exegesis of Psalm 110:4 in Hebrews 7:1-28 refers to the narrative of Melchizedek in Genesis 14.

The form of Hebrews is also influenced by the use of the rhetorical device of *synkrisis* (comparison) and the use of the "more or less" type of *a fortiori* argument. In order to show the superiority of a person or object, that person or object may be compared with an outstanding specimen of the same kind. Hebrews show the infinite worth of Jesus by comparing him with outstanding institutions and figures (angels, Moses, Melchizedek, etc.). The "more or less" argument is essentially the same as that used by the Rabbis with the designation *gal-wahomer* ("light and heavy").[10]

The attempt to outline Hebrews in a definitive way has met with no general agreement. Proposals are based on the major exhortations (seen as standing at the end of the major sections (1:1-4:13; 4:14-10:31; and 10:32-13:17)); the Christological ideas of the writing; the distinction between the hortatory and Christological parts: or on the basis of the scheme of Greek hortatory address. Alexander C. Purdy explains that "no outline can do justice" to the interrelationship of the author's ideas, particularly because of the "subtle and skillful way in which he prepares his readers for the exposition of Jesus as High priest (in 2:17; 3:1), for the discussion of 'God's

10. See Bruce, pp. xlvii-lii and George A. Kennedy, *New Testament Interpretation Through Rhetorical Criticism*, pp. 23, 89.

rest' (in 3:1, 18), and for the Melchizedek speculation (in 5:6, 10; 6:21)."[11]

The different historical situations and the different outlines suggested by commentators constitute not only evidence of the complexity of the Book of Hebrews, but also evidence that different readers — even critical readers — "concretize" or "actualize" Hebrews in light of their own psychological set and historical and sociological situation. Hebrews invites readers to interact with the text to relate the text to their own needs in the very process of reading.

A most interesting illustration of the fact that readers "actualize" the Book of Hebrews from their own perspective and structure the contents from their own actualization is seen in the case of Ernst Käsemann who published a major work on Hebrews in the late 1930s. Käsemann saw clearly that "all the utterances in Hebrews culminate in the description of Christ's high priestly office." It is because Hebrews is ultimately concerned with the question of the surety of obtaining the heavenly homeland that Hebrews is directed toward the message of the heavenly high priest in the form of a final word. But the *basis* for the statements of Christ's high priestly office "which supports and purposefully articulates the individual parts" comes "from the motif of the wandering people of God." Käsemann, therefore, takes Hebrews 3:7-4:13 as the point of departure of Hebrews. "Hebrews intends to show the Christian community the greatness of the promise given it and the seriousness of the temptation threatening it. For this reason, it sets before its eyes the picture of Israel wandering through the wilderness."[12]

In reflecting years later upon his writing of the book, Käsemann acknowledged the influence of his situation at the time of writing.

> In three years of work (an arduous task for the pastor of a large blue collar congregation), I gathered the material with which,

11. Alexander C. Purdy, "The Epistle to the Hebrews: Introduction and Exegesis," p. 580.

12. Ernst Käsemann, *The Wandering People of God*, pp. 17-18, 235, 240.

> during a four week imprisonment in 1937, I was able to compose the first draft of the version which was completed the following winter .... By describing the church as the new people of God on its wandering through the wilderness, following the Pioneer and Perfecter of faith, I of course had in mind that radical Confessing Church which resisted the tyranny in Germany, and which had to be summoned to patience so that it could continue its way through endless wastes.[13]

The outline which follows is offered not to enable readers to by-pass the active reading which the author of Hebrews expects but to suggest one way of organizing the result of reading and actualizing the content.

Outline of Hebrews

I. Introduction: The Son and Angels 1:1-2:18
  A. God's Final Revelation in His Son 1:1-4
  B. Christ Higher than Angels 1:5-14
  C. Admonition 2:1-4
  D. Subjection of the World to the Son — the Way of Suffering 2:5-9
  E. The Pioneer of Salvation made Perfect through Suffering 2:10-18

II. Participation in the House of God and in the Rest along the Way 3:1-4:13
  A. Christ's Faithfulness over God's House as Son Compared with Moses' Faithfulness as Servant 3:1-6
  B. The Rejection of Jesus More Serious than the Rejection of Moses 3:7-19
  C. The Promise of Rest Remains but It May be Forfeited 4:1-10
  D. Exhortation 4:11-13

III. The Nature of the Son's High Priesthood 4:14-7:28
  A. Christ's High Priesthood as Encouragement to His People 4:14-16

13. Käsemann, *Kirchliche Konflikte*, Vol. I, p. 17. Cited in *The Wandering People*, pp. 12-13.

- B. Christ's Qualifications as High Priest 5:1-10
- C. Readers' Qualifications and Challenge 5:11-6:12
- D. The Steadfastness of God's Promise 6:13-20
- E. Christ the Perfect Eternal High Priest according to the Order of Melchizedek 7:1-28

IV. The Superiority of the Heavenly Reality over its Earthly Copy 8:1-10:18
- A. The Heavenly Sanctuary and the New Covenant 8:1-13
- B. The Ministry of the Levitical Priests 9:1-10
- C. The Character of Christ's Sacrifice 9:11-10:18
  1. Secures Eternal Redemption 9:11-14
  2. Ratifies a New Covenant 9:15-22
  3. A Perfect Sacrifice 9:23-28
  4. The Reality of which the Old Order was a Shadow 10:1-10
  5. Perfection of the Sanctified 10:11-18

V. The Way of the Christian as the Way of Faith 10:19-12:29
- A. Privileges and Duties of Christians 10:19-25
- B. The Fate of the Willful Sinner 10:25-31
- C. Call for Endurance 10:32-39
- D. The Faith of Past Heroes and Heroines 11:1-40
- E. Exhortation to Faithful Endurance as Sons 12:1-29
  1. Jesus the Pioneer and Perfector of Faith 12:1-3
  2. Discipline as Sons 12:4-11
  3. "Lift your Drooping Hands and Strengthen your Weak Knees" 12:12-17
  4. The Earthly Sinai and the Heavenly Jerusalem 12:18-24
  5. "See that You do not Reject Him who Speaks" 12:25-29

VI. Concluding Admonitions 13:1-21
- A. Ethical Injunctions and Examples 13:1-8
- B. Genuine Christian Sacrifice 13:9-16
- C. Call for Obedience and Prayer 13:17-19
- D. Prayer and Doxology 13:20-21

VII. Postscript 13:22-25
- A. Personal Notes 13:22-23
- B. Final Greetings and Benediction 13:24-25

Bibliography

Commentaries

Barclay, William. *The Letter to the Hebrews: Translated with an Introduction and Interpretation.* The Daily Study Bible. Rev. Ed. Philadelphia: Westminster Press, 1976.

Bowman, J. W. *Hebrews, James, I & II Peter.* Layman's Bible Commentaries. Atlanta: John Knox Press, 1962.

Bruce, F. F. *The Epistle to the Hebrews: The English Text, with Introduction, Exposition, and Notes.* The New International Commentary on the New Testament. Grand Rapids: Wm. B. Eerdmans Publishing Co., 1964.

Buchanan, George W. *To the Hebrews: Translation, Comment, and Conclusions.* Anchor Bible. Garden City, N. Y.: Doubleday & Co., 1972.

Davies, J. H. *A Letter to Hebrews.* The Cambridge Bible Commentary. Cambridge: Cambridge University Press, 1967.

Fuller, Reginald H. "The Letter to the Hebrews." Pp. 1-27 in *Hebrews, James, 1 and 2 Peter, Jude, Revelation.* Proclamation Commentaries. Philadelphia: Fortress Press, 1977.

Héring, Jean. *The Epistle to the Hebrews.* Tr. by A. W. Heathcote and P. J. Allcock from 1st ed. in Commentaire du Nouveau Testament. London: Epworth Press, 1970.

Jewett, Robert. *Letter to Pilgrims: A Commentary on the Epistle to the Hebrews.* New York: Pilgrim Press, 1981.

Käsemann, Ernst. *The Wandering People of God: An Investigation of the Letter to the Hebrews.* Translated by Roy A. Harrisville and Irving L. Sandberg. Minneapolis: Augsburg Publishing House, 1984.

Manson, William. *The Epistle to the Hebrews: An Historical and Theological Consideration.* London: Hodder & Stoughton, 1951.

Montefiore, Hugh. *A Commentary on the Epistle to the Hebrews.* Harper's New Testament Commentaries. New York: Harper & Row, 1964.

Purdy, Alexander C. "Epistle to the Hebrews: Introduction and Exegesis." Pp. 577-763 in *Interpreter's Bible.* Vol. 11. Nashville: Abingdon Press, 1955.

Trentham, Charles A. "Hebrews." Pp. 1-99 in vol. 12 of *The Broadman Bible Commentary.* Nashville: Broadman Press, 1972.

Westcott, Brooke Foss. *The Epistle to the Hebrews: The Greek Text with Notes and Essays.* London: Macmillan & Co., 1892, 2nd. ed.

Special Studies

Barth, Markus. "The Old Testament in Hebrews: An Essay in Biblical Hermeneutics." Pp. 53-78, 263-73 in *Current Issues in New Testament Interpretation: Essays in Honor of Otto A. Piper.* Ed. W. Klassen and G. F. Snyder. New York: Harper & Row, 1962.

Bourke, Myles M. "The Priesthood of Christ." Pp. 55-62 in *To Be a Priest: Perspectives on Vocation and Ordination.* Ed. Robert E. Terwilliger and Urban T. Holmes, III. New York: The Seabury Press, 1975.

Dahl, Nils A. "A New and Living Way: The Approach to God According to Hebrews 10:19-25." *Interpretation* 5 (1951): 401-12.

Filson, Floyd V. *"Yesterday": A Study of Hebrews in the Light of Chapter 13.* Studies in Biblical Theology 4. Naperville, Ill.: Alec R. Allenson, Inc., 1967.

Horton, Fred. L., Jr. *The Melchizedek Tradition: A Critical Examination of the Sources to the Fifth Century A. D. and in the Epistle to the Hebrews.* Cambridge, Mass.: Cambridge University Press, 1976.

Johnsson, William G. "The Pilgrimage Motif in the Book of Hebrews." *Journal of Biblical Literature* 97 (1978): 239-51.

Käsemann, Ernst. *Kirchlische Konflikte.* Vol. I. Göttingen: Vandenhoeck und Ruprecht, 1982.

Kennedy, George A. *New Testament Interpretation Through Rhetorical Criticism.* Chapel Hill and London: The University of North Carolina Press, 1984.

Koester, Helmut. *Introduction to the New Testament.* Vol. II. *History and Literature of Early Christianity.* Philadelphia: Fortress Press, 1982.

———. "New Testament Introduction: A Critique of a Discipline." Pp. 1-20 in *Christianity, Judaism and Other Greco-Roman Cults: Studies for Morton Smith at Sixty.* Part One. New Testament. Ed. J. Neusner. Leiden: E. J. Brill, 1975.

____. " '*Outside the Camp*': Hebrews 13:9-14." *Harvard Theological Review* 55 (1962): 299-315.

Lo Bue, Francesco. "The Historical Background of the Epistle to the Hebrews." *Journal of Biblical Literature* 75 (1956): 52-7.

Manson, T. W. "The Problem of the Epistle to the Hebrews." Pp. 242-58 in *Studies in the Gospels and Epistles*. Ed. M. Black. Manchester: University Press, 1962.

Moody, Dale. *The Word of Truth: A Summary of Christian Doctrine Based on Biblical Revelation*. Grand Rapids: William B. Eerdmans Publishing Co., 1981.

Sowers, Sidney G. *The Hermeneutics of Philo and Hebrews. A Comparison of the Interpretation of the Old Testament in Philo Judaeus and the Epistle to the Hebrews*. Atlanta: John Knox Press, 1965.

Vanhoye, Albert. *A Structured Translation of the Epistle to the Hebrews*. Rome: Pontifical Biblical Institute, 1964.

2

God Speaks in His Son

Hebrews 1:1-4

Frank Stagg
Professor Emeritus
The Southern Baptist Theological Seminary, Louisville, Kentucky

Hebrews begins powerfully with a stylistically-honed sentence, four verses in English but one long, periodic sentence in Greek. It is thematic for the whole writing, whether a letter or sermon. It declares that (1) the Son of God is the focus for God's culminating word and work, both God's self-disclosure to us and God's saving action for us; and it declares (2) the superiority and finality of the Son for the revelation of God and for our salvation. This packs much into one long sentence. The rest of Chapter One and, in fact, the whole letter explicate and apply the perspectives and claims of this opening sentence.

This opening sentence of four verses is known stylistically as a "period" or "periodic sentence." To us, a period is a dot marking the end of a sentence. Originally, a "period" was a sentence itself, a carefully balanced sentence where expansions of the subject and predicate were introduced and carried along in such a way that the sentence ended with one carefully chosen word. Both the Gospel of Luke and Hebrews begin with such a stylistically deliberate periodic sentence (Lk. 1:1-4; Heb. 1:1-4). Listen to the opening, periodic sentence in Hebrews:

> In many measures and in many manners of old, God having spoken to the fathers in the prophets, upon the last of these days has spoken to us in a Son, whom he placed heir of all, through whom also he made the ages; who being the reflection of his glory and the mirror image of his essence, carrying all things by the action word of his power, having made cleansing from sins, sat down at the right of the majesty in the heights, by so much becoming better than the angels as one who inherited a name! (My translation.)

Revelation as Personal and Progressive. Can you imagine a preacher today beginning a sermon with an adverb followed by a conjunction and two more adverbs? That is precisely how Hebrews begins in its Greek original: "In many measures," "and," "in many manners," "of old," only four words in Greek.

The intention of these opening words is to affirm the limits and varieties of the way God has spoken to his people from time to time before Jesus Christ. If God cared only to speak, he could speak his mind once for all in one uniform and final way. That God has spoken in many parts and in many ways is because of human limitations. Our text recognizes that where revelation takes place, there are two parties, God and people. God has spoken; but he spoke "to the fathers," and he spoke "in the prophets." Revelation is not unilateral or monologue. In revelation there is the divine side and also the human side. Revelation occurs only when God speaks and someone hears. Revelation moves progressively, all the way from "in many measures and in many manners" to "upon the last of these days, he has spoken to us in a Son." Revelation is person to person, not station to station. God is personal, and he addresses us as persons. In neither revelation nor salvation does God override the personhood of anyone. The Bible is not dictation taken down by a scribe or stenographer. Revelation is not God making a recording. Revelation is God speaking to persons in various ways and ultimately in his Son.

Revelation as Self-disclosure. Revelation is God's disclosure of himself to persons. Revelation includes information expressed in words, but it is more than the giving out of facts. In revelation, God gives himself to us. Information can be important, but we are not saved by information. We are saved only by a Savior. Salvation is in knowing God, not knowing facts about God. Jesus put it this way, "This is eternal life, that they should know thee, the only true God, and Jesus Christ whom thou hast sent" (Jn. 17:3). Saving faith is trust, not believing theological truths. Saving knowledge is knowing God, not knowing theology. Hebrews builds upon this understanding of revelation and salvation. That is why revelation is presented as reaching its final form only when God spoke to us in his Son.

Verse 3 employs two models to affirm that in the Son we know God: "the reflection of his glory" and "the mirror image of his essence." The Greek *apaugasma* can intend either "radiance" or "reflection," either idea suited to understanding the identity of the Son. As divine, the Son radiates from within himself the glory of God. The Son also reflects the glory of God, meaning that when we see the Son we see God as he is. What we see in the Son is what we would see in God were we able to look directly upon God. What the Son radiates or reflects is the "glory" of God. Glory is a biblical term for the character of God as reflected in what he does to save his people. This is the message implied in the angelic song in Luke's poetic story of the birth of Jesus: "Glory to God in the highest" (2:14).

The second model in verse three we render, "mirror image of his essence." Actually, "mirror image" is our paraphrase of the metaphor in Hebrews. The Greek term is our word "character." Originally *charakter* stood for an instrument for engraving or stamping an official seal, then it came to be used for the impression made by the instrument. *Charakter* thus implied the exact correspondence between the engraving instrument and the impression made upon wax or paper. In Hebrews, the Son is the *charakter* of God's very essence. "Mirror image" is a modern way to stress exact correspondence. However expressed in metaphor, Hebrews insists upon the exact correspondence between God and the Son in whom "in the last of these days" he has spoken. In sum, revelation as the self-disclosure of God reaches its ultimate expression in the Son, who radiates and reflects the character of God as Savior, this belonging to the very essence of God.

The Coming of the Son as Eschatological. Verse 2 introduces the eschatological frame for our text and for the whole of Hebrews. In the phrase, "in the last of these days," *last* renders *eschaton* in Greek. With other early Christians, the writer of Hebrews saw the days ushered in by Jesus Christ as "the last days" or the "end time." They expected an early return of Jesus, probably in their lifetime. In this time-table they were premature; but their essential view was sound. They were in fact living in "the last days." The age ushered in by the Son was the age toward which all the ages had moved. The *eschaton* had dawned. The ultimate dimension will be realized only when Jesus returns to bring both judgment and salvation to their final goal, but "the age to come" has already come in Jesus, "the Coming One."

The arrival of the *eschaton* with the Son meant that both revelation and salvation culminate in the Son. Thus, the readers are warned that it is unnecessary and futile to look behind or beyond the Son for God's word or his work, his speaking or his action.

The eschatological emphasis had a special meaning for the readers of Hebrews, for they were living in a time of crisis, with impending if not actual persecution (12:4). Hebrews probably was written during or soon after the Jewish-Roman War which erupted in A.D. 66, resulting in the destruction of Jerusalem and the Temple in A.D. 70 and the heroic struggle at Masada in A.D. 73. This was a war in which Jews fought for national survival, and lines were drawn closely. Christianity had been born and cradled in Judaism, and the war posed for Christians a most difficult choice. It posed a crossroads in their journey, or a point of no return. Would their basic identity be with a Jewish nation increasingly isolated in its brave fight for survival, or would its identity be with a new humanity transcending ethnic and cultic distinctions?

Hebrews seems to see the readers as tempted to revert to their Jewish origins or at least to linger too long and too closely to the cultic side of their Jewish heritage. Hebrews insists that there must be no lingering or looking back. They are to move on in commitment to Jesus Christ as the reality and the finality of all that was anticipated in their Jewish heritage. Under the pressures of war for national survival, Judaism was withdrawing into its own shell, especially under the Pharisaic ideal of their being the people of the Mosaic Law. With increasing inclusion of Gentiles in the Christian movement, the relationship with their Jewish past was increasingly difficult. The destruction of Jerusalem and its Temple was a devastating blow to cultic practice. In such a crisis, where were the readers of Hebrews to find their identity and their direction? Hebrews is loud and clear; it is in the Son in whom God has spoken and acted with finality and in whom God's very essence is radiated and reflected. Christians are to see themselves as a pilgrim people, ever marching onward as a people of Exodus. The vision is introduced here at the outset, and Hebrews moves to its climactic call to pilgrimage in its closing chapter:

> So Jesus also suffered outside the gate in order to sanctify the people through his own blood. Therefore let us go forth to him outside the camp, bearing abuse for him (13:12-13 RSV).

Hebrews thus offers the same assurance and issues the same call found in Mark 13, both written in view of the same crisis. Jesus warned his disciples that Jerusalem and the Temple would be completely destroyed, but he assured them, "The end is not yet" (Mk. 13:7). City and Temple would go, but God was not gone. God's work would go on, and they must go on with God's work. This is the assurance and commission also in Hebrews.

Heir of All. Verse 2 affirms the Son as "heir of all" and the agent in creation. The implication of his being "heir" is clearer in 1:6, where he is God's "firstborn" Son. In Jewish society, the "firstborn" son had special birthrights. Inheritance and authority were ideas belonging to that of "firstborn." This may be the key to the very last word in the Greek "periodic sentence" ending in verse 4, the word "name." The Son has among his advantages over angels the inheritance of a "name." As "firstborn" son, he inherits a name from the Father. The elusive reference in verse 4 to "a name" is followed by the probing question: "To which of the angels did he say at any time, 'My Son you are, I this day have begotten you,' and again, 'I shall be to him a Father, and he shall be to me a Son' "? (v. 5). Sandwiched between "name" and "firstborn" is the Father/Son emphasis in verse 5 stressing not only the relationship but the oneness in estate and authority. What belongs to the Father belongs to the Son, whether possessions or name. This serves the major purpose of Hebrews to point to Jesus, the Son of God, as the focus for revelation, salvation, and the ongoing journey necessary to his people.

Linked to the term "heir of all" in verse 2 is the acclaim, "through him whom also he made the ages." This is resumed in 1:10-12, where the Son is addressed as "Lord," an Old Testament term for God, and where the Son is seen as "in the beginning" having created the earth and the heavens. The contrast is between the Son as the Agent in creation and creation itself. The heavens and earth are temporal, once not having been and now subject to passing away, like an old, discarded garment. They pass away, but the Son abides. The Son was there "in the beginning," and he will abide forever. Hebrews was addressed to people whose world seemed to be passing away, both Jerusalem with its Temple and the securities once felt within the cultic rites of Judaism. The Church now faced the prospect of being cut off from such past securities. Hebrews points them to the Creator as their security, not the fragile creation or anything within it. The city to which they once looked was vulnerable to Roman sword and torch, and the inclusion of Gentiles could mean their exclusion from the community out of which they came. They are pointed to "another city" and, most of all, to One who died outside the gates and with whom they must be on a perpetual Exodus.

Having made Cleansing from Sins. Transactional atonement may be implied in verse 3, "having made cleansing from sins." Supporting evidence for this idea appears in such passages as 9:14,28 and 10:12. The idea of cleansing from sins (not Sin) is explicit, but the further idea of a sacrifice offered the Father to satisfy his rights or demands goes beyond what is explicit and is precluded by the recognition of the oneness of the Father and the Son, the Son being the reflection of God's glory and mirror image of his essence.

The Son is not seen as overcoming reluctance in the Father but as bringing to completion the intention of the Father. Both continuity and fulfillment in saving action are stressed. This accords with the view throughout the Bible that God has inherently the authority and disposition to forgive sins and save sinners. The Old Testament is replete with this view. Psalm 51 is unsurpassed in its message that God awaits only a contrite heart before his cleansing and healing mercies pour out savingly. The term "Savior" appears 24 times in the Greek

New Testament, eight times for "God" as our "Savior." The term "Savior" appears interchangeably for "God" and for "Christ." The deity of Christ does not compromise monotheism, the oneness of God. The very name "Jesus" means JHWH Savior (Mt. 1:21). Jesus Christ is Immanuel, "God with us," not God against us.

Deeply embedded in Hebrews is the perspective in which salvation occurs as one participates with the Son in his own pilgrimage and victory. In 2:11f Savior and saved are both out of one; they are alike. In 5:8-10 Jesus is the "cause" (*aitios*), i.e., the catalyst of salvation through suffering to those who obey. This implies existential involvement of saved with the Savior, not an event as in itself saving. In 6:19-20 Jesus is "Forerunner" (*prodromos*) who leads us into the Holy of Holies, i.e., into the presence of God, where one finds one's true humanity. In 7:24-25 Jesus is the eternal priest who brings us to God. He does not go to God as a substitute for us. He enables us to enter into the presence of God. In 12:2 Jesus is the pioneer and perfecter of our faith, effecting something within us, not just for us.

The concern in Hebrews is pastoral, not primarily for systematic theology. Where sacrificial language is borrowed from cultic rites, the concern is to affirm the supremacy, sufficiency, and finality of Jesus Christ for our salvation and ongoing life. The readers are not to look back to cultic sacrifices, for they have in Jesus the true high priest, sanctuary, and sacrifice. In the final analysis, the Son saves sinners not by some external event as a transaction to satisfy the Father but by effecting change in the sinner's disposition, direction, and destiny.

Superior to Angels. The periodic sentence with which Hebrews begins is brought to its conclusion in verse 4 with the declaration that the Son has a name better than that of the angels. The rest of the chapter argues that the Son is greater than the angels. Seven texts are drawn from the Old Testament to support the Son's supremacy over the angels. The name "Son" is given to one alone, not to any of the angels (v. 5). The angels are to worship the Son, not the other way around (v. 6). The angels are reduced to servant roles, like winds and flames of fire (v. 7). The Son is addressed as "God," whose throne is forever and whose scepter is righteousness; and he is God's anointed, set apart and above his fellows, presumably angels (vs. 8-9). The Son is from the beginning; he is creator of earth and heaven; and he will remain when all these are gone (vs. 10-12). The Son sits enthroned at the right hand of God, the seat of power, whereas angels are ministering spirits sent in ministry to those about to inherit salvation (vs. 13-14).

Why is it so important to Hebrews to argue that the Son is greater than angels? One possibility is that there may have been a tendency to worship angels, a problem dealt with in Colossians. Probably the problem lies in another direction. At this time there was a rabbinical teaching that the Law was given to Moses through the mediation of angels. Paul reflects this tradition in Galatians 3:19. Since the Law of Moses was basic to cultic practices, it was important to Hebrews to show that the Son is superior to angels, hence superior to the Law given to Moses through the angels. To Hebrews, just as God spoke "in many measures and in many manners" of old to the fathers "in the prophets," so he spoke to Moses through the limited means of the angels. Now God has spoken with finality in his Son. Since the Son is superior to angels, what God has spoken in his Son takes precedence over all other speaking, whether in the prophets or through angels. Rather than looking back to cultic codes and practices of Mosaic tradition, the followers of Jesus are to look to him for God's definitive word. He is superior, sufficient, and final for revelation, for salvation, and for their ongoing journey.

3

The King is at the Door

Hebrews 2:5-18

William A. Lawson
Pastor, Wheeler Avenue Baptist Church, Houston, Texas

He is a successful executive in a Dallas insurance firm. He lives in a beautifully-furnished home, drives an expensive car, and regularly wears expensively-tailored clothes. But his most precious souvenir is not ivory from Africa nor a tapestry from Singapore. It is a common mop. While he went to school, he worked nights as an orderly at a huge public hospital which served the poor. One Friday he swapped shifts with a day worker, and cursed himself for the inconvenience of the arrangement. Suddenly the hospital was in an uproar; all the surgeons and the administrators and nursing staff were rushing about in a frenzy. Someone yelled at him to bring his mop and bucket and all the towels he could find to the Emergency Ward. A patient had been shot, and was bleeding profusely.

"So what else is new?" he asked a fellow-worker. "There is always somebody shot, and bleeding. Why all the excitement about it?" He remembers his fellow-worker grabbing his arm and yelling, "Come on and quit asking dumb questions! This is not an ordinary shooting — this is the President of the United States!" So he joined the frenzy as an entire hospital staff worked to save the life of President John F. Kennedy in Dallas' Parkland Hospital. He mopped blood and medications and sweat for the dying President, and shared the despair of the hospital when the President died. That night he confiscated the mop from the supply room of the hospital, and speaks of it almost as if it were a sacred relic. He has met dignitaries from all over the world since then; but will never forget the Friday afternoon when the President came to the public hospital in Dallas, Texas, and he mopped his blood from the floor.

That story is the central message of this passage from the letter to Hebrew Christians. Mankind is living in frustration and defeat. And into his misery comes God himself, to identify with man's frailty and despair. But God does much more than identify with man's lowliness — through Jesus Christ he rescues battered mankind and elevates him to a place of high honor.

The writer of Hebrews (Paul? Luke? Barnabas? Apollos?) tells his readers that God has always wanted to communicate with us. He has spoken to us through both earthly and heavenly agents — through prophets and angels. But his most complete revelation of himself to us is through his son, Jesus Christ. Prophets and angels could give us fragments of a portrait of God, but Jesus is the perfect portrayal, the absolute messenger, the matchless advocate. He is the consummate high priest, because we do not have to earn the privilege of going to his throne — he comes into the lowly place where we mop our floors and curse our circumstances and wet our pillow with tears.

The greatest music has simple themes that can be hummed or whistled. The finest art often depicts very ordinary subjects. And what is profound in this passage is the simple skeleton of ideas it contains. There are four — let's glance at them.

God had big plans for us

The writer of this letter was somebody of great culture and of elegant rhetoric. He was also someone who understood well the divine nature of Christ. Notice that until now this writer has not even mentioned the name of Jesus (the first time he calls it is in this passage, 2:9). Instead he identifies him as God the Son, terrible in his pre-incarnate glory, one with the Father, very God of very God. So with his elegant mastery of Greek language and of Hellenistic thought, he begins his letter by calling God the Son the perfect, final, and ultimate revelation of God. John tells us that God the Son was the agent of creation. "All things were made by him; and without him was not any thing made that was made." And the Son made man in the image of God. The author quotes Psalm 8:4-6 in Hebrews

2:6-8. God the Son fashioned his human being with a royal flourish, designed to be a ruler, to control the rest of the created universe. He "crowned him with glory and honor," and set him over the works of God's hands. He "put all things in subjection under his feet."

Psalm 8 is not a poem about the greatness of God, nor about the Messiah. Even the term "son of man" which appears in verse 4 of that psalm is part of a poetic couplet referring to "man" in a double question:

> What is man, that thou art mindful of him? and the son of man, that thou visitest him?

The entire psalm is a hymn to the glory which God gave to man. God's original intention for his highest creature was that he should have God-like qualities of creativity, of judgment, and of dominion. God would endow man with those qualities and then tell him to run the universe. No other creature was so endowed; no other creature was so assigned. God had given his primeval couple two simple orders, immeasurably grand in their sweep: reproduce yourselves and take control of creation.

> Be fruitful, and multiply, and replenish the earth, and subdue it: and have dominion over the fish of the sea, and over the fowl of the air, and over every living thing that moveth upon the earth.
>
> — Genesis 1:28

Remember that high assignment and then re-read Hebrews 2:5-18.

God had big, big plans for us. We would engineer the march of the seasons, and calculate the orbits of the planets. We had power to control the productivity of the vegetation of the earth, and to direct the destinies of every creature that breathed, rewarding or punishing or sustaining according to the behavior of the creature. No volcano could erupt nor river flood its banks unless we ordained it. We were the chief executives of the creation, answerable only to the Creator.

So why isn't it like that now?

We blew it

The writer of our passage reduces the most disastrous tragedy in history to a single comment in verse 8.

> But now we see not yet all things put under him.

That is putting it mildly! Man can control neither nature nor other human beings. You and I live in a world where natural catastrophe is as common as changes in the moon, and where injustice, brutality, and human conflict are too routine to be newsworthy. The man who was intended to control nature's productivity now must run from drought or flood or fire or starve to death. The high creature who was ruler of the living beings can now be destroyed by a virus he cannot even see.

We have often softened the concept of sin into the simple disobedience of a mischievous child. Its effect on man is far more devastating than that. There is no measurement for the distance man fell when he sinned against God. The pitiable and vulnerable shell we are now, shrunken by poverty, scarred by sickness, decimated by wars and by crime, twisted by greed and lust and hate, bears almost no resemblance to the majestic ruler of the universe God first installed in Eden. Man did not descend from innocence to experience — he fell and fell and fell, past all the creatures high and middle and low, to a depth which made him beneath the snakes of the ground. He became the cause for which God cursed everything that surrounded man — "cursed is the ground for thy sake," thundered the angry Creator.

How badly did we blow it? Would you believe even worse than the fall of Satan was the fall of man? Look again at Psalm 8, a bit more closely now. Verse 5 proclaims that God made man "a little lower than the angels," and then adds that God "crowned him with glory and honour." We can tell that something is wrong here, because even if we had not read Hebrews 2, we would have known that man could not be at the same time "lower than the angels" and yet "have dominion over the works of thy hands;" nor have all things put under his feet. We cannot recall God giving such a status to angels. But in case there is question, Hebrews 2:5 clearly states it for us:

> For unto the angels hath he not put in subjection the world to come, whereof we speak.

The conflict is cleared up when we realize that our English translations are not completely accurate. They are accurate translations of the Greek Old Testament, from which much of the Masoretic text is drawn. But they do not accurately quote the original Hebrew in which the Psalm was written. The word used by the psalmist is not mal'ak, which is invariably the word translated "angels," but Elohim, which literally means "God." Now read the verse and you get a clearer picture of how high man was in the beginning:

> For thou hast made him a little lower than God, and hast crowned him with glory and honour.
>
> Thou madest him to have dominion over the works of thy hands; thou hast put all things under his feet.

Man was not "lower than the angels;" the angels have always been God's servants. Man was made to be an overlord, to manage the worlds, to be in God's image and after his likeness, not to be God's messenger but God's child, the heir to Deity! Lucifer fell from being a chief servant to being an unredeemable adversary. But man fell from a position higher than that of Lucifer at his most glorious to a depth that would make the fallen Satan stronger than man. If we are no match for the inanimate forces of nature, then surely we cannot compete with the cunning and powers of the Prince of Darkness.

We blew it — *real* bad!

So God designed a masterpiece of a creature, and used himself as a model, made his creature only a little lower than himself, and made him boss of the created universe. And then, with all that going for us, we decided to write our own job description in opposition to God's task for us. And we lost our status under God and the magnificence of the mind and body we had been given.

That's the bad news. But the writer of the Hebrews says there is good news.

Our creator came to the scene of our wreck

The writer of Hebrews has already described God the Son in terms more lofty than any place in the Bible except possibly the first chapter of the Gospel of John. God the Son is Creator, the brightness of God's glory, the express image of his person, and as the one who upholds all things by the word of his power (Hebrews 1:2, 3). When God determined the specifications of his highest being, "in our image, after our likeness," it was God the Son who turned out the finished product. And when the man chose to rebel against God and stripped his gears, threw his rods, and slammed headlong into sin, the Father reached into the files of Heaven, pulled out the plan of salvation that had been laid out before the foundations of the world, and sent the Son to the place where man lay, virtually totalled out. Man is at the moment much lower than the angels, weaker than nature, more frail than the animals, less productive than the plants of the ground, and no match for Satan. Man would not seem to be worth repairing at all —ready for the cosmic junkpile.

Verses 9 and 10 tell us that the Father reduced the Son from omnipotent, omniscient, omnipresent God, consubstantial with the Father, to a status like that of man, subject to the laws and powers of nature, available to the wiles of Satan. But God made his Son at the same time inheritor of man's frailty and of the Father's virtue. He came, innocent of sin, that he might take our place in the Death Row of history. We had one thing going for us that Satan does not have — God would redeem us from our sins. No angel has that privilege!

The miracle of the grace of God is in its very expansiveness. You and I might forgive an oversight or an error; but not so easily deliberate malice or cruelty. We can be gentle with the clumsiness of a child; but may have much difficulty exonerating one who with evil forethought abuses his neighbor — and may do it repeatedly. But God sees all these types, loves all these types, and is willing to restore all these types to his own bosom. God the Son, who is finally identified as Jesus in verse 9, is willing to call us his brothers, children of the same Father:

> For both he that sanctifieth and they who are sanctified are all of one: for which case he is not ashamed to call them brethren.
> — Hebrews 2:11

How is it possible to look at the style of God and still cling to the selfish manner of fallen humankind? As low, as filthy, as vile, as guilty as we are, God is willing to take upon himself a body like our own corruptible bodies, to endure the weaknesses of mortal man, and to take our place on the Death-Tree. We are too good for some classes of people. We will not have fellowship with many we have stereotyped as inferior or untouchable. We may have no forgiveness in our hearts for those who have been found guilty, even if there is no evidence they are pathological. There are so few people we will take to ourselves! But Jesus comes into our leper colony and warmly embraces us with our rotting flesh. If God's Son shows me anything at all, it is the incalculable grace and mercy and compassion of God. And if that grace, that mercy, that compassion compel me to do anything, it is to show my love for God's Son by loving others as he has loved me.

Think about the grace of God next time you are mulling over the strategies by which you will spit back at somebody who has misused you. Remember how we have been forgiven next time some poor wretch begs you for mercy or for understanding. Our Creator did not send angels to the scene of our wreck — he came Himself.

The real crux of this passage is the way in which he came.

He rescues us by his own suffering

We are not surprised if the writer of this letter describes God the Son as our high priest. That seems a fittingly aristocratic position for the Creator-Redeemer. But after the awesome and magnificent description of him as being equal with the Father and as possessing all the attributes of full divinity, it is difficult to digest the other image of him as a suffering servant. All our gallery of portraits of heroes is scandalized here. It makes sense if he saves us with his strength, rescues us with his cunning, redeems us with his hosts of heavenly warriors. But what kind of hero takes the place of the victim and bears his abuse and his pain? The Jews to whom this letter was written surely had more noble ideas of what the Messiah would be like whenever he appeared. And yet whatever image they had of the Messiah, the writer of Hebrews reminds them that God had already given them abundant preview in the Psalms and in the Prophets. In verses 12 and 13 he quotes from Psalm 22:22, from Isaiah 8:17, and from Isaiah 8:18. All of these texts depict the Saviour as one who suffers, not as a conquering warrior-king. It is not enough to affirm that God comes to the place of our calamity to find us. The plan of salvation which God devised for us adds to that portrait the suffering of the Savior as the central feature of the salvation he brings. He "took not on him the nature of angels;" he became a child of Abraham, a lowly Jew who must bear the stigma of having made the labors of Moses more difficult, the pleas of Samuel vain.

This image of salvation, then, the sophisticated writer of Hebrews hurls at his Greek-oriented readers. Such an image surely shocked them. For the Greek idea of the gods was of detachment, of aloofness, of utter lack of concern with the sufferings of their human subjects. On the lonely splendor of Mount Olympus, they received the adoration of mortals with a kind of cold disdain. Against this backdrop the writer paints a tear-drenched picture of a God who hurts for us, Who cannot be satisfied in his glory while we struggle against our punishment, and who ultimately absorbs our hurt himself by suffering in our stead.

What shall be our response to such a Savior? We marvel at his compassion; we glorify him as he bears our pain; we can sing endless hymns to his beauty and his love. But none of these explain what he is doing. Remember that Jesus is our Creator, who fashioned us to be in the image and after the likeness of God. What he does we are to emulate. If he is the light of the world, he expects us to be the light of the world. He performs mighty works before us, and challenges us to do great works, because he returns to the Father. He stoops to wash the feet of his disciples, reminds them that he is their Lord and Master, and then challenges them to wash one another's feet as he has done for them. He is the Good

Shepherd; and he tells us that if we love him we must demonstrate it by feeding his sheep. Eloquent sermons and masterful recitatives about the love of God do not scratch the surface of what our high priest expects of us. He wants us to display our newly-redeemed nature by caring for the universe as he had once assigned us to do.

If there is hunger, we must provide food. If there is sickness, we must bring healing. Where man is in despair, we must speak the word of hope. Wherever injustice oppresses the weak or aggrandizes the powerful, we must be the voice of the weak and the goad in the side of the merciless. The thrust of these fourteen verses is that God gave us a high and noble purpose, and through the suffering of his only begotten son he has provided reconciliation to himself, and a return to that high and noble purpose for which we were born. All the cathedrals in the world, and millions flocking to them to thunder anthems of praise to the God of hosts will not please him as much as a cup of cold water given by a child of God who knows the misery of thirst.

The gods at their coldest are detached from the masses. God at his most beautiful is the Son of Man, weeping for the sins of Jerusalem. Man at his most corrupt is self-centered, living entirely for his own profit or power or pleasure. Man at his finest is identified with his neighbor as Jesus Christ identified with us. Some day we will rise again above the status of angels!

4

Christ the Supreme Guide

Hebrews 3:1-6

Virginia C. Barfield
Visiting Instructor of New Testament
Southeastern Baptist Theological Seminary, Wake Forest, North Carolina

Back in my undergraduate days I enjoyed collecting posters. I especially liked nature scenes — sunrises/sunsets, mountain scenes, calm lakes, waterfalls. And best of all, I liked serious quotations that depicted the deep side of life. One poster that I had hanging on my wall is still etched in my memory. The scene was an aerial view of a winding country road at night. The headlights of a lone car brought only a minimum of light to the picture; but without those headlights, the winding curves would have been totally unrecognizable. The words on the poster — "Life is a journey" — are definitely overused and trite, but in those days they spoke reality to me. The poster served to remind me that I was on a journey of discovery and that, even though the road seemed dark, there was enough light available for me to carry on.

I do not know who wrote the book of Hebrews. Furthermore, I do not know who the people were who first heard or read it. I do not know where they lived. But there is one thing that seems clear to me about the author, the recipients (let us call them "The Hebrews"), and their relationship with each other. The Hebrews were wandering — they were moving about randomly without clear direction or purpose. They had begun to experience discouragement in their journey in the faith. They were wandering in their faith much as the children of Israel had wandered in the wilderness. They were in need of encouragement and re-direction. The writer of Hebrews sought to meet this need by holding forth Jesus Christ as an example and source of encouragement and direction. Jesus was the pioneer of their salvation (2:10), the pioneer of their faith (12:2). It was Jesus to whom the wanderers should look. It was Jesus who was able to illumine the winding road along which they were stumbling.

"Come, my brothers and sisters, let us this day consider Jesus." Such is the call of the writer of Hebrews 3:1-6. Direction and encouragement for the journey were provided in these words. Let *us* study them carefully for they may provide us with guidance for our own wanderings.

Hebrews is a Christological tractate. It focuses intently on Jesus and thereto directs the attention of "the wanderers." The word "consider" which the author uses is the Greek *katanoein.* It means "to reflect on," "to consider deeply," "to fix the eyes of the spirit upon." The sense of the command is this: "Stop moaning and grumbling about how difficult your situation is. Turn your vision back to Jesus. Meditate on him. Reflect on what he has done."

In the previous passage (1:5-2:18), Jesus is portrayed as superior to the angels. Here and in the following verses, the author pictures Jesus as superior to Moses. Moses, the figure who led the Israelites on their wilderness journey, was faithful. He was one of the most revered of all the Hebrews. Jesus stands above Moses, but Moses is in no way depreciated. Moses' faithfulness to his task is upheld. His task was that of a servant, to testify to those things which would be revealed later through Jesus, God's own son. Moses was a faithful servant: Jesus, a faithful son. Herein is the superiority of Jesus. Jesus, apostle — the messenger sent by God — and high priest, is the one to whom we must look when our travels are difficult, when we seem to lose our way, when we need a guide.

And who are the people who are instructed to look to Jesus? It is in this third chapter of Hebrews that the writer of the book first identifies his audience. In verse one, the audience is specified as "holy brethren who share in a heavenly call." The ones who are exhorted to turn their eyes back to a consideration of Jesus are members of the Christian community. The author counts himself as one of these people, one of "God's house" (v. 6). And it is within this community of God's house that the Hebrews can find encouragement. Wandering without a clear sense of direction can be a rather lonely enterprise. The discouragement can be lessened when we realize that we do not travel the road alone. This is the point that the writer makes.

Those who read the passage are immediately struck by its emphasis on community. We are those who have received a heavenly call. We are part of God's house. We are the holy brethren who have lost our way and are stumbling and grouping for redirection. And how we all do seem to stumble and grope!

Perhaps we have lost our way because of over-zealousness. We are working so hard and doing so much that we have forgotten the basis of our efforts. We, as the community of God, are so busy planning and executing those plans that we have lost our way in a maze of projects, programs, and procedures. We are stumbling as we try to meet all the external requirements of the faith. We are called to remember our foundation, to "consider" Jesus.

Or maybe we have begun to lose direction because we, like the Hebrews, have come upon hard times. It seems that the Hebrews had been through some persecution (10:32ff). The faith they embraced had caused them to suffer. We do not often find ourselves in actual situations where we are persecuted for our beliefs, but we do find ourselves in situations that test our faith. For example, there are some of us who are intent on living our faith. We are trying to live as Christians in a world that seems at times to be not very Christian. In spite of our attempts to "be Christian," we find ourselves frustrated by unrealized dreams and lost expectations. We spend our lives rearing children and looking with anticipation to the retirement years — the years that we can enjoy the spouse we love so very much. Suddenly, the spouse dies. Our dreams of "happy ever after" are gone. Loneliness and grief fill our days. And we do not deserve this. We were faithful and committed.

Or, we have tried hard to listen to God's voice as we prepare for our life's vocation. After years of diligent preparation we land a job — a position that must certainly be God's will. But we are not happy. The task is not what we expected.

Surely God would not call us to such an unpleasant chore. We have been so faithful. We do not deserve this.

Or, we have lived a "good" life — taken care of our bodies, eaten wisely, gotten plenty of exercise. We have treated our bodies as the very temple of God, only to have our faith shattered by those dreaded words: "I am sorry. Your sickness is so advanced. There is nothing I can do."

These are the times that can shatter our dreams, challenge our faith, and make us wonder if the journey is worth the effort. These are the events that make us doubt and question and wander. This is the kind of wandering that begs for a sense of community in which to put it all back together.

The author allies himself with the Hebrews and reminds them that they are all related as brothers and sisters in the household of God. They are sanctified by Jesus and have one origin (2:11). Although their pains, their persecutions, their doubts, their wanderings may be individual, their hope and encouragement are communal. The courage and steadfastness to withstand these days would come from their community and its efforts to meditate on Jesus. The writer says: "Come, my brothers and sisters, let us this day consider Jesus."

What, then, is the purpose for this communal meditation on Jesus? We must join together and fix our eyes on Jesus in order that we might be God's house. And we can be God's house only "if we hold fast our confidence and pride in our hope" (v. 6b). The way to overcome the discouragement and loss of direction which the Hebrews experienced was to dig their feet in, to hold fast, to persevere in the present moment.

This last portion of verse six contains the key to overcoming spiritual wandering. The verb used here is *katekein.* Its basic meaning is "to hold fast," "to retain faithfully those attitudes and ideas which have carried one thus far." In this sense, the writer is repeating the emphasis of verse one. He is saying: "Consider your faith in Jesus which has sustained you up to now. Hold fast to your belief in what Jesus has accomplished on your behalf as high priest." In a more technical sense, however, this verb can be used as a nautical term meaning "to steer towards." The emphasis here would be that of looking ahead, of casting one's sights on the future goal

—the goal of the promised rest which awaits the faithful (4:1,9). This interpretation in the technical sense of the word is reinforced when we notice what it is that they should hold fast. They are instructed to hold fast their confidence and pride in their *hope.* Hope, the expectation of something good, is that towards which the Hebrews should certainly steer. Perhaps both the root ideas of *katekein* are pertinent and are conveyed by this command. The Hebrews are told to solidify their faith by holding fast to what they have acknowledged and to steer toward their future expectation. A glance back and another forward can alleviate the problem of tunnel vision which sees only the frustration and discouragement of the present.

The Hebrews are also instructed to hold fast to their confidence. The word translated as "confidence" is *parrhesia.* Etymologically, the word means "freedom to say all." Its central emphasis is openness to the public. The confidence called for here is not a subjective, internal, positive outlook. It is a courage, a boldness, a positive outlook that verbalizes itself. It is a faith that "goes public." The writer in 3:1 has, in effect, told the Hebrews to stop moaning and grumbling and to turn their vision to Jesus. Here in verse six, the positive command is "Be bold. Speak forthrightly of your faith and the certainty of your hope." The cure for loss of direction in one's faith journey is in the outlook that speaks boldly and publicly even in the midst of frustrating times.

"Come, my brothers and sisters, let us consider Jesus" and let us be God's people and "hold fast our confidence and pride in our hope." Are we twentieth century Hebrews who have lost our way? Are we struggling along in this journey called life? Have we become despondent and discouraged because our dreams are not coming true? Are we in danger of losing our confidence and our hope? Let us not despair. We are not journeying on a winding country road with no headlights to show us the way. We have Jesus, the pioneer of our faith. Let us look to him. And let us look forward to the promise of rest. Let us boldly proclaim our faith in Jesus' work and in the certainty of our hope. In the midst of our wanderings, let us hold fast to our faith. This is the encouragement the songwriter Tom

Fettke offers in the following chorus:

Be strong, be strong,
Be strong in the Lord.
And be of good courage
For He is your guide. ("Be Strong in the Lord")

Let us cease from our wandering and move forward in the assurance of our faith. Let us *truly* be the house of God for each other and for the world!

5

The Tragedy of Unbelief

Hebrews 3:7-19

Chevis F. Horne
Pastor Emeritus, First Baptist Church, Martinsville, Virginia

People who do not learn from their history are doomed to repeat the follies and tragedies of the past. History is a masterful teacher but often we are dull students. We fail to read the signs of warning that history holds before our eyes and we do not hear what history says to us despite the fact its voice is almost deafening in its power.

The author of Hebrews was afraid that his generation of early Christians were poor students of history, that they were about to repeat the folly of the wilderness generation that perished while almost on the border of the Promised Land. The common link between that fateful generation and his own was unbelief which was tragic in its nature. "So we see that they were unable to enter because of unbelief" (3:19). He was afraid that a similar fate would overtake his generation.

Warned By History

The author quotes Psalm 95:7-11 which reflects two sad stories in the life of Israel: the rebellion in the wilderness where Moses struck the rock in anger (Ex. 17:1-17; Nu. 20:1-13), and the poor response to the report of Joshua and Caleb, who were two of the twelve men sent into Caanan to spy out the land (Nu. 14:1-25). The underlying tragedy of the two stories was unbelief.

As the author looked at that lost generation in the wilderness he saw unmistakably the heavy hand of God's judgment. God swore in his wrath that "they shall not enter my rest."

It is interesting that the author looked to history to find God's judgment. That tells us a lot about our faith. Judaism and Christianity are historical religions which means that God acts, both in judgment and grace, in history. There is where he meets us, where he tells us who he is. There is where he judges us, and there is where he saves us. He doesn't save us out of history but in it.

The author is concerned with God's judgment which is an inescapable reality. God's judgment is basically two things: the working of moral law and God's personal wrath.

God has built his ethical nature into the moral structure of the universe. These moral laws are as much a part of his universe as are the physical laws, and they are just as unrelenting and demanding.

If I live in the valley and along the slopes of a mountain, I have to come to terms with nature's laws if I am to survive. If I am careless I can freeze in the blizzards and snows of winter, and I can be washed away by the floods of spring when the rains come and the snow melts. Just so with the moral laws. I have to come to terms with them. They have a cutting and jagged edge, and I can destroy myself on them.

God's judgment also has a personal side. He is a God who hates evil. He becomes angry when men and women violate his laws, rebel against him, and injure each other. "I swore in my wrath." The emphasis here is on the personal element, yet we do violence to reality when we do not see the working of moral law as a part of the judgment scene.

God's judgment did not let them reach their destination. He said he swore in his wrath that "they shall never enter my rest." The term rest is a beautiful, poetical word for the Promised Land. "For you have not as yet come to the rest and to the inheritance which the Lord your God gives you" (De. 12:9, RSV).

The term rest had a special appeal to wandering nomadic people to which the wilderness generation belonged. They dreamed of reaching their rest after being freed from the blasting winds, excessive heat, burning thirst, and exhaustion of the desert. They envisioned their new land with houses, vineyards, and green pastures not far from their dwellings. After a long journey with its hardship, privation, and weariness they would finally reach their home. It would indeed be a rest.

But the sad thing is that that generation never made it. They died in the wilderness almost on the border of the Promised Land. We still feel the agony of it. The long years have not destroyed its pathos.

Uneasy About The Present

The author was uneasy about his own generation. He was afraid they might commit the follies of the wilderness generation and thereby come under the judgment of God. There were signs which were omens of bad things to come. He spoke of drifting away (2:1), of neglecting so great a salvation (2:3), of commiting apostasy (6:6), and of carelessness in attending the worship of the church (10:25). In our Scripture lesson he spoke with concern "lest there be in any of you an evil, unbelieving heart, leading you to fall away from the living God" (3:12). He was afraid that history might be repeating itself, that the same fate that overcame the wilderness generation might overcome his.

When the author thought of history repeating itself, he did not envision a kind of mechanical repetition like revolving doors going round and round. His view was not that of Ecclesiastes. "What has been is what will be, and what has been done is what will be done; and there is nothing new under the sun" (Eccles. 1:9). Many of the ancient world saw history that way, a kind of cyclical recurrence. He saw history as a forward movement. It was going somewhere, not just repeating itself. History was humanity on the march under the providence of God. Even in the wilderness, although maybe much of the wandering was going round and round, it was a forward movement with the rest as the end of the journey. Yet, the author knew that the mistakes of the past could be repeated. He was afraid that was what was happening to his generation.

His contemporaries had as their end a rest, too. (See 4:1). It was the rest of the new age which Christ would bring to its completion with his return, and it was the rest of heaven. It was too great to miss!

What could make the present situation so tragic was that they had an advantage over the generation that perished in the desert. What if they did not make the most of it? While

Judaism provided an access to God, it was shadowy, broken, and unfulfilled. The Christ event had changed things, fulfilling Judaism. Christ had brought a new day where God was seen in a clearer light. And Christ had made God more accessible.

Christ was greater than Moses. Moses had been a worthy servant of God, but Christ had been his faithful Son. Therefore, Christ had done that which Moses never could have done. As wonderful as the Exodus under Moses was, Christ had made possible a much more significant one.

The original Exodus was the highlight of Israel's history. It was the loftiest peak in her range of experience. When a little Hebrew boy asked his father the meaning of their history, the father's answer always was: "We were Pharaoh's salves in Egypt; and the Lord brought us out of Egypt with a mighty hand (De. 6:21, RSV). God had taken them when they were helpless slaves in Egypt and had delivered them into freedom.

While you do not find deliverance from political bondage in the New Testament, you find a greater exodus. Christ has set us free from the two ultimately enslaving powers over human life — sin and death. Paul could write: "For the law of the Spirit of life in Christ Jesus has set me free from the law of sin and death" (Rom. 8:2).

Sin and death are back of all our historic bondages, be they social, racial, political, or economic. Christ has gotten back of all these enslavements and delivered us from the bondage that lies back of bondage.

With this great new advantage, it would be such a tragedy for the author's generation to fail. It is bad when tragedy comes upon a people who walk in shadows and broken light. It is worse still when it overcomes a generation that walks in the light of full day.

The Tragic Nature of Unbelief

It was because of unbelief that that far-away generation was not able to enter its rest. The same kind of unbelief could keep the author's generation from reaching its destination. Such unbelief was unmistakably tragic. But what kind of unbelief was the author speaking about?

There were basically two kinds of doubt or unbelief — intellectual and moral.

Intellectual doubt is common in our time. It is of the mind. The experiences of life seem to cast a shadow over God. Often faith is made shipwreck, for example, on the treacherous shoals of evil and suffering of which we have so much in our world. If God were perfectly good and all-loving, as well as having unlimited power, why would he allow so much destructive evil and agonizing pain? That is likely the most difficult question the human mind has ever asked.

Jesus was gentle with intellectual doubt. You remember the father of an epileptic boy, coming to Jesus, half-doubting and half-believing, at the base of the Mount of Transfiguration. Jesus was so accepting and uncritical of him. "If you can!" Jesus said, "all things are possible to him who believes" (Mark 9:23).

Moral doubt is much more serious, and Jesus is much more severe on it. While intellectual doubt is of the mind, moral doubt is of the will. In moral doubt we set our wills against the will of God, we seek to thwart his purpose. We rebel against him. Given light we choose darkness, with freedom before us we choose bondage, and offered life we choose death. Moral doubt is evil.

The unbelief that threatened that early generation of Christians as well as the generation from the past was moral, not intellectual. The author spoke of how the earlier generation "saw my works for forty years." They had evidence of God's grace and providence. The shadow of doubt lay, not over their minds, but across their wills. The author spoke of how they rebelled, how they hardened their hearts. He therefore urged his generation not to have "an evil, unbelieving heart," that they be not "hardened by the deceitfulness of sin."

What would avert the great tragedy threatening his generation? The author suggests four things.

First, realize the urgency of time. "Today, when you hear his voice, do not harden your hearts as in the rebellion."

Time is the very essence of life and they had so little of it. Their lives were slipping away like sand running through the hour glass. They were called to decision. Decide now! Tomorrow may be too late.

Again, they were to hear what God was saying. This admonition leads us to the very heart of our faith. Our God has not remained silent. He has spoken!

Pascal told of how the silence of the heavens frightened him. How much more frightening would be the silence of God. What if his word had never pierced the mystery and darkness of our world? Our life would be a nightmare. But he has spoken, in ways we can understand, through persons and historical events. His voice has about it a human accent. He has spoken in greatest clarity and greatest finality in Jesus of Nazareth.

Further, they were not to harden their hearts as in the rebellion. They must not be guilty of moral doubt. They must not set their wills against the will of God. They must not turn from God who is light into the paths of darkness. They must not turn from God who is life into the ways of death. They must not "fall away from the living God." They must know that in the doing of God's will is their peace.

Finally, the author stresses the importance of the church in enabling them to hold onto the faith that keeps them in a vital relationship with the living God. When he says "but exhort one another every day," he is speaking about the fellowship and worship of the Christian church. If they were to avoid the fate of that tragic generation, they must be practicing Christians and a part of the Christian fellowship. The church was indispensable. They had no option here if they were to remain faithful to God and strong in their relationship with each other.

We need to stress again the importance of the church. It is not an appendage to the Gospel, it is a part of the good news. We say the church cannot save us and that is true. But it is equally true to say that we could not have been saved without the church. It has been the keeper and proclaimer of the Gospel, and without it we never would have heard the good news of salvation. And a Christian cannot survive and grow into maturity without the church.

I have always found the behavior of a fish out of water to be interesting. It flounces with such vigor and vitality, but it is the flounce of death. The water is its habitat and it can't survive unless it gets back into the stream. The Christian is like that fish. The church is his or her habitat, and he can't survive outside its life.

There is one more question: What does the author mean by faith? He tells us what he means by unbelief, but he is not so explicit when it comes to the matter of faith. He, later in his book, will give what is likely the most unique definition of faith in the entire New Testament: "Now faith," he wrote, "is the assurance of things hoped for, the conviction of things not seen" (11:1, RSV). Faith is many faceted, and in our passage he looks at it from a little different angle. As I have said, the author doesn't explicitly define it in our passage. But he comes nearest to it when he writes: "For we share in Christ, if only we hold our first confidence firm to the end." He seems to be more in the mainstream of faith as envisioned by the New Testament: personal trust in God that continues steadfast to the end.

This passage is very pertinent to us and our time. It would be a kind of redundancy to keep on stressing how it speaks to us. It has a built-in relevance. Let us heed what it says!

6

Sabbath Rest

Hebrews 4:1-13

C. Welton Gaddy

Senior Minister to the University, Mercer University, Macon, Georgia

When in Jerusalem on the eve of Shabbat, I like to go to the Wailing Wall. With awe and appreciation, I delight in watching the impressive assemblage of worshipers there. Young and old come — rabbis robed in black and children clothed in bright shorts, women who move quickly to the right side of the wall and men who studiously take their places on the left, individuals who stand alone praying as if they are the only persons in the world and groups chanting litanies in unison. At sundown a horn signals the beginning of the Sabbath and the ending of all superfluous activities. Policies prohibiting smoking and picture-taking are enforced. Stores close. Personal movements are monitored. Worship is expressed. The Sabbath has arrived and is observed.

No doubt, many persons label such a strenuous observance of the Sabbath as the vestigial remains of an Old Testament practice that should have been abolished long ago, an unhealthy hangover from an intoxication with legalism. Such a rigorous reaction to the Sabbath seems a bit of an unnecessary bother to a mindset in which worship is considered a come-and-go affair and Sunday only one more segment of a seven day week. "We are beyond all of that ritualistic foolishness in our spiritual pilgrimages toward maturity!" Maybe, but, I think not.

Honestly, I find something attractive, challenging, and instructive in this rigid Sabbath observance. In Jerusalem, I have the feeling that I am watching persons dedicate their undivided attention to an important dimension of life which my homeland neighbors well-nigh have lost. Perhaps the

Orthodox Jewish observance of the Sabbath does tend toward an extreme. If it does, perhaps our casual recognition of Sunday tends toward another extreme — quite possibly more unhealthy.

The Sabbath was a principle in the mind of God long before it was a day on our organized calendars. To be more to the point, emphasis on the Sabbath concept is present both in creation and redemption.

From the very beginning, God's instruction to his people was, "The Sabbath day is a day of rest dedicated to me" (Exodus 20:10); "Observe the Sabbath and keep it holy" (Exodus 20:8). Characteristically, God modeled what he commanded. That is his compassionate nature. Thus, God implemented in creation that which he expected from the created: "And on the seventh day God . . . rested . . . so God blessed the seventh day and hallowed it" (Genesis 2:2-3). Provision of the Sabbath was an integral part of creation.

Pious Jews responded to the divine demand for Sabbath observance with well-intentioned actions that moved toward excess. Positively, the day of rest was designated also a day of worship. Then, however, efforts to avoid abuse led to abuse. Prohibitions related to Sabbath observances proliferated. Soon the real meaning of the day was buried under the debris of legalistic interpretations of the day. The Sabbath was transformed from a divine provision for the good of people into a religious institution to be protected by people.

Jesus offered the proper corrective to this situation. As a devout Jew, Jesus regularly made his way to the synagogue on the Sabbath (Luke 4:16). However, as the Savior of the world, Jesus boldly clarified the meaning of the day: "The Sabbath was made for the good of man; man was not made for the Sabbath" (Mark 2:27). Implicit in the harshness of people's reaction to Jesus' assertion was an insight into the strength of the Sabbath tradition. The simple point enunciated by Jesus contributed substantially to a controversy that ultimately cost Jesus his life. Ignoring the significance of the Sabbath truth as discussed by Jesus can cost us our lives!

Eventually a radical change in primary worship days took place within the Christian community. After the ascension of

Jesus, Christian believers began to worship on Sunday rather than on Saturday. After all, Sunday was the day of resurrection, the occasion of the Lord's first appearance after the grave. Surely Sunday was *the* day of celebration. Thus, Sunday came to be known as "the Lord's Day" — a day for praise, prayer, a fellowship meal, the Lord's Supper, proclamation and commitment; a day of worship. Interestingly enough, though, for members of the primitive community of faith, Sunday was not a day of rest.

The earliest Christian disciples existed as a minority sect. For most members of Greco-Roman society, Sunday was a work day. Thus, Christian worship was scheduled early and late — at dawn before work and late at night after work. That arrangement did not change significantly until the fourth century. In the year 321 the Emperor Constantine, with less than Christian motives, declared Sunday to be a public holiday. At long last, Sunday could be observed by Christians as a day of rest as well as a day of worship. Precisely at this point in history many of the regulations previously associated with Saturday, the Sabbath, were applied to Sunday, the Lord's Day.

In time, as Christianity grew in popularity and Christians moved toward a more influential, if not majority, status in society, laws were passed to assure civil recognition of Sunday that paralleled the old spiritual recognition of Saturday. When Christians actually gained control of a government, tendencies existed to enact legislation which would force within society a general compliance with special Christian beliefs. So-called "blue laws" were instituted. Sunday would be a day of worship by divine decree and a day of rest by civil law.

In recent years, injustices in the legal situation related to Sunday activities have been corrected. Unfortunately, though, in the process of needed alterations in legislation, the significance of "a day of worship and rest" has been sabotaged. Please understand my total lack of desire to impose personal religious beliefs upon anyone else by means of a civil law. However, know as well of my conviction that a recognition of the principle of Sabbath rest is crucially important for the good of society as well as for the health of individual persons and the glory of God.

Of course, Sabbath rest as commended in the ministry of Jesus and invited by the Book of Hebrews involves far more than physical relaxation and spiritual worship, much more than a day of the week or a date on a calendar. At stake here is the promise of a pervasive peace, a comprehensive security, available every day, indeed, throughout eternity. A commitment of life to Christ rather than a ritual of Jewish tradition is most essential if this rest is to be experienced.

To disciples of Christ belong the assurance of a means of rest unrelated to activity, a comfort for the soul whether working, praying, or playing. The testimony of the Old Heidelberg Catechism accurately treats the truth involved. "What is your only comfort, in life and in death?" the document inquires. Then follows the powerful, restful response, "That I belong —in body and soul, in life and death — not to myself but to my faithful Savior, Jesus Christ." Hear. Hear.

Observance of a Sabbath Day, valuable in itself, encourages recognition of the larger truth regarding Sabbath rest. True education in this regard will result in meaningful participation. We need not only to understand Sabbath rest, we need to experience it.

SABBATH REST REGULATES THE RHYTHM OF LIFE — INCORPORATE IT!

Rest is as necessary to life as work. Rest was not an afterthought of God, no delayed addendum on the agenda of creation, no compromise for weaklings. No! Rest is an integral part of God's plan for his people, a divine intention in creation as well as a compassionate provision in redemption.

Jesus embodied the rhythm of life perfectly. Study the patterns of his ministry: engagement and retreat, encounter and escape, relentless ministry and restful solitude. That is the model. Only when work and rest are held in proper balance is real health possible. That is the rhythm of life. That is the rhythm required for life.

Surely all of us are aware that a major contributing factor in many contemporary illnesses is that dreaded phenomenon known as stress. Talk with anyone about it. Calendars are full. Schedules are crowded. Expectations are excessive. Increased sales figures must be reported. Additional business meetings must be convened. Appointment times must be expanded. More letters must be written. Social contacts must be multiplied. Almost everyone is overextended.

Energies are drained. Heads hurt. Blood pressure soars. Hearts fail. Anxieties abound. Depression develops. Hostility is hoarded. Anger erupts. Individuals panic. Business partners fight. Families disintegrate. The problem is frustratingly cyclical. Stress creates an inability for an individual to relate to other people in a manner that would ease stress. Stress prevents the very kinds of activities that could alleviate stress. Unchecked and unhelped, persons under stress grow worse and worse until life snaps.

Please do not think it simplistic to suggest that a critical need exists for persons to embrace the divinely intended rhythm of life. Sebastian DeGrazia has posited that the inner health of a society can be judged by its members' capacity to do nothing, to rest. Individuals who can relax know a security which allows their thoughts to go wherever they will. Obviously, these persons are at peace with themselves and with God. How all of us need times in which our souls can catch up with our bodies!

So, what is wrong? Could it be that we are not at peace with ourselves and thus afraid of a rest that allows us to get in touch with ourselves and thus become restless? Or, maybe we are too much victimized by that dogged phenomenon of competitiveness: "I do not have time to rest, I simply must get ahead." Certainly economic concerns have taken their toll on Sabbath rest. We are eyewitnesses to, if not participants in, a rabid commercialism which seeks to squeeze from every hour of the day work to be done by employees and coins to be spent by customers. A gross insatiable gnawing in our economic stomachs is symptomatic of a deadly hunger that will be satisfied only at the expense of a loss of life in both patient and doctor.

Every person needs a Sabbath. People require rest. What is true for an individual is also true for a family, a business, and a society.

When does our society rest? When does our community rest? When do you rest?

Incidentally, I am not so sure but what everyone confronts the priority of Sabbath rest eventually, either as a celebrant of it or as a victim devoid of it. Wayne Oates first helped me discover the implicit truth of Psalm 23. "He makes me lie down in green pastures." Notice carefully: "He *makes* me lie down!" Do you see? Rest is an integral part of the rhythm of life. Either we lie down for rest or life lays us down.

Imagine wandering in the wilderness for forty years. Think of the discomforting, tiring complications of such a trek. Little wonder that arrival in Canaan was viewed as arrival in the land of rest. Against the backdrop of that realization, the writer of Hebrews announced that God continues to provide such rest, but more — incredible rest for the weary *today.* All any one of us needs to do is to accept it.

Sabbath rest regulates the rhythm of life: incorporate it.

SABBATH REST RECOGNIZES THE NECESSITY OF FAITH — CELEBRATE IT!

As a distinctive day, Sunday has great symbolic value, a pointer to the transcendent dimension of life, a reminder of the necessity of faith. When this day is really different from all other days, persons realize that life involves more than an office routine, household chores and periodic entertainment. Spiritual aspects of life get highlighted and the need for attention to them acknowledged.

We need Sundays. Someone has said that a person without God cannot bear the burden of himself or herself. Perhaps that is why a sometimes-medical professor at Harvard recently included worship on his list of four essentials for life. We need Sundays.

Without the resource of strength found in faith, life closes in on us. Apart from an extension of ourselves, an offering of ourselves, in Christian worship, we see life in too narrow a context, on too flat a level. Problems press us. Strength dwindles. Resolve fades. We are on our own — to make our own day, to face difficulties on our own, to work out our own salvation.

Contrast that situation, if you will, with an observance of Sunday, an indulgence in Sabbath rest, a regular acknowledgment of faith in a context of Christian worship. It is like opening a window and letting the fresh air and bright sunshine of springtime flood into a room which has grown dark and musty from years of closure. Christian worship puts us in touch with new vistas of purpose, new sources of strength and new dimensions of joy.

Ironically, the very people who feel that they simply do not have time for regular experiences of worship are the very people most in need of regular experiences of worship. Oh, I know that they are hustling — aren't we all? — working a second job, trying to make ends meet, playing hard at relaxation, traveling with the family, fixing up a country house, watching each installment of the National Football League on television. However, the one experience which they feel that they can most afford to miss is the very experience which they cannot afford to miss.

How can we live without regular worship? That which we give up for it is that which we find in it. What we lose to participate in worship is what we discover in the participation. Honestly, I do not know a single invididual who worships regularly — not attends worship, but worships regularly — who does not have more purpose, joy and meaning in life than any individual who forfeits worship.

For me, personally, worship is absolutely essential. Sometimes in the course of a week I find myself literally longing to get to a meaningful hour of corporate worship,to be with other believers in a context of praise, confession, commitment and renewal. Of course, sometimes I am tired and do not feel like making the effort for such an experience. Occasionally, I have to force myself to move toward participation. Even so, however, I can tell you honestly that almost inevitably in the course of the hour I change. Maybe it is in the swell of the organ's expressions of praise or through a quietly spoken call to worship or by means of the crescendo of a choral anthem or in response to the clarity of a word of Scripture or during my involvement in a confessional prayer — the exact moment varies though the outcome remains the same — that my soul is nurtured and I come alive, anew. Faith is strong once more. How can we live without worship?

Sabbath rest recognizes the necessity of faith: celebrate it!

Sunday is the first day of the week. Krister Stendahl has made an interesting point in that regard. We do not work all week in order to get to Sabbath rest. Rather, Sabbath rest is the source from which life begins. Our involvement in rest and worship is not a reward for work; it is a reason, even a resource, for work. Sabbath rest is not inactivity at the end of a journey, it is strength for the journey. Life begins with celebration.

Ancient Jewish apocalyptic writers often referred to the first day of the week as the "eighth day." This is the day on which the new creation begins, the day of resurrection. How true! We dare not miss this day. We need its rest and we need its worship. God commanded it. Our souls cry out for it. The eighth day.

Sabbath rest regulates the rhythm of life: incorporate it! Sabbath rest recognizes the necessity of faith: celebrate it!

Rest, welcome, needed, longed for rest — rest for the weary, for the troubled, for the anxious, for the grieved, for the restless. Rest! And, worship — worship which takes us beyond ourselves, puts us in touch with the transcendent God, gives us new strength, reinforces hope, nurtures faith. Worship!

Faith. Redemption. Rest. Worship. Yes. All are promised. Each can be claimed. Let it be so for us, dear God. Let it be so for all of us.

7

Our High Priest: New and Different

Hebrews 4:14-5:10

John Sullivan
Pastor, Broadmoor Baptist Church, Shreveport, Louisiana

"Out of sight, out of mind," may be an old adage, but it presented a tremendous problem for those who followed Jesus Christ once he had left this earth. The absence of Jesus from his followers had to be solved if Christianity was to remain a viable option for men's loyalties. If they could just see Jesus ; if he would only display himself, it would make it much easier to believe in him. With this in mind, the author of Hebrews approaches the reality of Jesus against the backdrop of the Old Testament tabernacle. Just as the high priest went behind the veil of the Temple to do his work of redemption, our author pictures Jesus as going behind the veil of heaven to do his work of redemption. Though the people could not see the high priest behind the veil, they could see and benefit from the evidence of his work. With these things in mind about the high priest, the author sets out to validate Jesus as the eternal High Priest.

It is surprising that the Old Testament does not give a clear picture of the Messiah as the high priest. It is in the New Testament, and especially in the book of Hebrews, that we find this exciting concept. The high priest was, beyond question, the most important person in the religion of Israel. The writer desires the church to conceptualize that the high priest is also the most important person in their religious faith. It was the function of the high priest to enter into the presence of God on behalf of the people. It was always considered a dangerous thing in the Old Testament to approach God. For some, it meant death. In Exodus 33:20, God says to Moses, "You cannot see my face and live." In Judges 6:22 — 6:23 when Gideon discovered he had been speaking to the angel of the Lord, he was reassured, "Do not fear. You shall not die." The high priest was permitted to come into the presence of God to make atonement for the people, but even for him it could be dangerous. He wore bells on his robe so that the people could hear him as he did his work. Some commentators indicate that he even had a rope tied to his leg so that if the bells ceased to ring, he would be dragged from behind the veil of the temple. No other person was allowed to go in to bring him out. It was always a risk of life to enter God's presence in the Old Testament.

God lives in covenant relationship at all times. This covenant relationship is very special. Parties enter into covenant with a sense of stimulation, spontaneity, and simplicity. Certain conditions must be allowed in covenant relationships. The writer wants us to see, as Christians, that Jesus Christ is our high priest because of the new covenant with God. When New Testament believers are disobedient and break the commandments of God and hence break the covenant, it will not be the sacrificial system that is administered by the high priest that brings us back into relationship. It will be the high priest. In Jesus, the high priest did not make a sacrifice — the high priest was the sacrifice! This makes our high priest new because he is eternal and different because he became the sacrifice. The glory of the church is that Jesus is the perfect eternal sacrifice and priest.

Much like the world of the first century, we also live in a "prove it and I'll believe it" day. The world is lumbering at the door of the church asking, "Where is this Jesus of whom you speak? If he is alive as you say, produce him so that we can see, feel, and hear." The world about us still walks by sight and not by faith. They cannot see beyond the visible. There is a story told about Joe that illustrates this conclusion. Joe was a downtown janitor. Every day precisely at 12:00 o'clock, his lunch hour, Joe walked across the street into the church, knelt at the altar, and said very simply, "Jesus, this is Joe," stayed for only moments, and left. One day while crossing the street to the church, Joe was struck by a car. He was taken to a ward at the hospital. It was a very noisy and vulgar place. In the midst of it, things began to change because of Joe's attitude, spirit, and rapport. Finally things had changed so much that one of the nurses asked, "Joe, I do not understand how you have maintained such credibility and peace. Will you tell me?" Joe's simple explanation was, "It is because every day, precisely at 12:00 o'clock, Jesus comes to my bed and says, "Joe, this is Jesus." If the high priest concept advanced by the author of Hebrews ever reaches the optimum in our lives, it will be because we also hear, "This is Jesus!" The theme of Hebrews is "Access to God." Jesus, as the high priest, affords us that access. We have no reason to fear or to hesitate in our faith and service.

What are the Qualifications for the High Priest?
(Hebrews 5:1-4)

The qualifications for the high priest run along two lines of insistence: Jewish insistence and God's insistence. The ancient Jewish priesthood had always come from the tribe of Levi and the family of Aaron. At the time of Jesus, the Jews still insisted that the high priest be a pure-blooded descendant of Aaron. Historically, the only time this was violated was during the interbiblical period when the leader of the nation also served as High Priest.

God insisted on certain other qualifications for the high priest. It was here that many of the Jewish high priesthood failed. They were not willing to meet God's demands for the essential nature of covenant relationship.

Does Jesus Qualify as the High Priest?

The question is now posed, does Jesus qualify as a high priest? An obvious answer is, not by Jewish qualifications. Jesus was from the family of David and the tribe of Judah, not the family of Aaron and the tribe of Levi. However, this is precisely what the writer desires to relate — Jesus qualifies on the higher level. Our author is not interested in genealogy or ancestral pedigree. He is interested in essential religion stripped of trappings!

There is the absolute necessity for a new and different high priest. A high priest who would have no need of making atonement for himself. A high priest who would not need to make atonement annually for others. A high priest who could establish an eternal covenant. A high priest who could make a perfect sacrifice that would satisfy the demands of a righteous God toward sin. A high priest who was fully divine and fully human.

Our author takes the reverse order of the qualifications he has given in Chapter 5:1-4 to show that Jesus qualifies. He sets forth these necessities:

1. The high priest must be able to appropriate the things of God in relation to the sin of man by his gifts and sacrifices.
2. The high priest must be able to show compassion (the gentle touch) to sinning man by his identity with man's suffering.
3. The high priest must not take the office to himself. The office comes by the authority of God.

The writer, in considering the essentials of priesthood, begins with fellowship and relationship between God and the priest. Because sin disturbs the relationship between man and God, the high priest must be able to deal with sin. This is why he makes the gifts and sacrifice (5:1). The sin offering made on the day of atonement was the most special celebration on the calendar of Israel.

The high priest must also qualify in matters pertaining to or in matters in which men are responsible before God. The high priest is not qualified just on his precise performance of ritual details. Hebrews 5:2 tells us that he must have inward feelings about the external work that he performed in behalf of others. The word "compassion" (5:2) means "to bear or touch gently." It is a blend of patience and love. This quality of life kept the priest from becoming indifferent to the point of indulgence. It also spared him from becoming sentimental to the point of impotence. The high priest adjusted himself to deal with the abuses of Israel toward God in a gracious and feeling manner. He could not afford the exasperation and indignation which could easily have come because of Israel's rebellion and self-centered conduct.

Every high priest had to be acceptable to God before the sacrifice he made would be accepted by God (5:3). The obligation of making sacrifice for himself was not only the legal demand of the Levitical law, it was to come as well from the pressure of conscience. This made his offer for his own sins more than a ceremonial regularity and an atoning ritual. The high priest had to establish his own forgiveness in order for God to sympathize and deliver the people. This qualification of the high priest enabled him to sympathize without compromise.

Another qualification for high priest had to do with authority and call. No man could, of his own volition, be a valid high priest (5:4). Just as God had called Aaron, he called his successors. If a man were to take his office by personal assumption, it would indeed be an arrogant assumption! An arrogance that would continue to mark the exercise of the office. But when man is appointed by the authority of God, there can be no arrogance.

The writer now begins to document that Jesus is the High Priest (5:5-10). He begins his proof by letting us know that God chose Jesus (5:5). As proof of that choice, our author begins at the baptismal experience of Jesus. Christ did not glorify himself — God glorified him. To be anointed high priest was always an honor. However, in the case of Jesus, it was glorious. God called him his Son! The inference of this seems to be involved with the process of perfection. Christ was divinely appointed. He was not only suitable to be son but also to be priest. His priesthood is based on his sonship. God's design was to lift to eternal union redemption through his Son and the accomplishment of that redemption. Our writer chose to point this truth against the historical setting of the high priest.

The entire conduct of the life of Christ was an outward expression of his perfect character. As the Son of God, he was without flaw. Therefore, he did not need to make sacrifice for himself. G. Campbell Morgan, in his book *The Crisis of the Christ*, says that his character is perfect: "Whether at the feet or the funeral, with the scholars or the simple, whether with the adults or the children, whether in loneliness on the high height or amid the crowds that surged about Him, He was ever acting in response to the impulse of the spirit of power, the spirit of love, and the spirit of discipline."

Having been chosen of God, the priesthood of Jesus refused dependency on genealogy or tribal identification. He had become the High Priest of God as the perfect sacrifice. In the Son of God there was perfect union of the divine and the human, thus elevating the sacrifice to a new dimension. Jesus can bring together God and man because he is God and man!

To validate the fact that Jesus had not chosen the priesthood for himself but had been chosen of God, the writer uses two passages from the Old Testament, Psalm 110:4 and Psalm 2:7. The same God who claimed Jesus as Messiah and Son also claims him to be High Priest after the order of Melchizedek. Jesus was not priest by descent but rather by authorization and self-sacrifice. This makes the high priesthood of Jesus superior to any other. You cannot return to anything you have ever known that is as good as Jesus, is the insistence of our author.

In a very real sense, the earthly life of Jesus is a demonstration of what God had already chosen in eternity. The events of Palestine and Calvary are those episodes which afford men an opportunity to see the character and nature of God.

In Hebrews 5:7-8, the writer takes up the second qualification of the high priest. This might well have been the ingredient most often missing in the life of the Levitical priest — that he must be able to bear with people without being annoyed to the point of becoming blind and calloused. He must have the ability to feel with the tender touch or to be compassionate. The compassion of Christ came as he learned the painful experience of obedience. He submitted himself to psychological rejection, social humiliation, as well as physical pain. In all likelihood, Hebrews 5:7 is a reference to Gethsemane. Even when Jesus knew that God had the power to deliver him from death, he chose not to exercise that power. Through his suffering, Jesus gained the ability to sympathize and to patiently bear up under the sins of others.

This concept of the patience of Jesus seems to be at the heart of the matter (5:8). By this, he executed a mighty change in the high priesthood and gave it full meaning. Even when enemies multiplied, misunderstanding about him became critical, and attitudes of opposition soared, there was no hostile and whining retaliation by our Lord. The temperament of his soul held on with calm ability in the midst of unbearable circumstances.

It is difficult for us to understand just how much Jesus suffered. For thirty years he waited. Charles Jefferson, in his book *The Character of Jesus*, speaks of this waiting:

> "Think of what this delay must have meant to Jesus. As man after man brushed by him on his way to success and renown, his soul must have been agitated. He too must have felt the fever to hasten on. Think of what his dream was and you will understand how it must have tugged at him and made the years seem interminable in drowsy, prosaic Nazareth. But he waited. At twenty-one, he said, Not yet. At twenty-five, Not yet. At twenty-eight, Not yet. It is in the twenties that the blood is hottest and the soul is most eager to get on. Through all the blazing years of youth Jesus waited in Nazareth. It was not until he was in his thirtieth year that he said to himself, 'The time has come.' "

The patience of Jesus was inexhaustible. Wherever he went, they watched him in order to trick him. He could not speak without fear of being trapped. Every action brought a new storm of criticism. He was misunderstood but he never complained. He was patient both with his enemies and his friends. His patience with friends was personified when he took a basin of water and performed the work of the ordinary —washing feet.

The final requirement and qualification for the high priest is found in the authorship of salvation (5:9). Salvation deals with forgiveness through sacrifice. In Hebrews 5:9-10, the author states that "Jesus was made perfect" and "became the author of eternal salvation." The Greek concept of perfect is not that of an abstract perfection. It has to do with function. A thing was perfect in the Greek mind if it functioned perfectly in the purpose for which it was created. Jesus is able to function perfectly as salvation because he is an eternal High Priest.

What are the Benefits of this New and Different High Priest?

The nature of Jesus Christ, though it was gentle and sweet, was also resolute and firm. Jesus had the courage to be himself. He was not an echo of his times nor of the religion of Israel. He could not be contained as a citizen of the first century. By living a life of perfection, he achieved a work unlimited by time, genealogy, or geography. In choosing to function for the purpose for which he was born, it meant Gethsemane and Golgotha. It meant that the world would hurl all of its energy at him with frantic force. In every instance where they sought to bring about compromise, they discovered he would not budge. He did not compromise his principles and consequently did not jeopardize his victory. He refused to be manipulated in his function even by his friends.

In his function as the perfecter of salvation, there was something inflexible about his will. Salvation could now be offered as eternal and perfect. Men can now come boldly to the throne of grace (4:16). The throne of grace is simply another way of saying the presence of God. We can do this due to the confidence we have in the ability of Jesus to forgive sin. His perfection allows his forgiveness to act upon the moral consequences of our sin. Out of this forgiveness or because of this forgiveness, loneliness is dispelled, self-contempt is erased, and mercy and love are honored (4:15a). We cannot undo our acts of sin. We can only approach the High Priest. The sacrifice of Jesus will forgive and transform the consequences of sin. Through his mercy, this transformation is accomplished.

In coming boldly or drawing near to God, we find timeless help through the compassion of Jesus. The presence of Christ as our High Priest should allow us to submit without reservation to the will of God. We will never come to the throne of grace with a difficulty that Jesus cannot understand (4:15b). His conflict with the problems of life and death were real. The pains of temptation were bitter. He understands because he has been there. Yet he did not sin. He had victory over all temptation and so can we. Jesus is as sympathetic as he is victorious. These things should give us confidence in his purpose, his power, and his provision as High Priest.

All mankind is in need of reconciliation to God. Through alienation we have the feeling that God is our enemy. At our most hostile moments, we feel that we are the enemies of God. The only religious faith available to us is the faith of repentance. We approach the throne to produce harmony and unity out of a life of discord. It has been well said that in Christ we are reconciled to God, to each other, to ourselves, and to our responsibilities.

In our time of need, we must come to the throne because love demands a sacrifice. Jesus, the High Priest, satisfies that demand. He suffered in love. There is no more difficult situation in life than the discord that happens because of man's sin. Reconciliation is the ministry of the High Priest who is both new and different. He is new because he is holy. He is different because he is righteous. He is a different kind of High Priest because the sacrifice will never need to be made again. He is different because the salvation he offers is eternal. He is different because he is approachable and gives us access to God. In Jesus we find the only instance of the High Priest being the sacrifice rather than making the sacrifice. That is different!

8

Christianity A *No Parking* Religion

Hebrews 5:11-6:12

E. Glenn Hinson
David T. Porter, Professor of Church History
Southern Baptist Theological Seminary, Louisville, Kentucky

Hebrews is full of "no parking" signs. In the view of the preacher who first delivered this sermon, Christianity is a "no parking" religion. To stand still is to slide backwards. To stop is to let salvation glide past. Worse still, to park is to put ourselves in a position of spiritual danger.

Have you read the "no parking" signs? "How shall we escape if we *neglect* such a great salvation" (2:3)? "Let us be fearful lest any of us seem to fail to enter into God's rest by letting the promises "lay there" (4:1), as the ancient Hebrews, even Moses, failed to enter the promised land on account of their hesitation as well as disobedience. "Let us approach *with boldness* to the throne of grace to receive mercy and find grace" (4:16). The word "boldness" is neon-lighted throughout this sermon (3:6; 4:16; 10:19-35).

Salvation is here. We can't park and wait for it to come to us. We have to get after it. We have to pursue it energetically. Salvation flows like a stream, and if we tie up at the dock, it may flow right on past. Stated in other imagery, salvation is the prize bestowed at the end of a race. Cheered on by a great throng of witnesses, we press on behind the lead runner, Jesus (12:1-3).

The biggest "no parking" sign in Hebrews is the passage on which this sermon is based, 5:11-6:12. In it the preacher chides and cajoles his hearers for spiritual sloth. They had had time to grow up and become teachers, but, alas, they were still babies in faith not yet on solid food. They were still on ABC's when they should have gone on to more advanced things. This could not be if the Holy Spirit had truly laid hold on them and worked them over. They would be producing good fruits rather than thorns and thistles.

Strong language? Indeed, yes. Enough so that the preacher relents a little in his critique. "But even if we speak like this, we are confident of greater things for you which pertain to salvation" (6:9). All, then, is not lost. The preacher only wants them to show the same eagerness to attain the goal they had shown in beginning this race. Christianity is not a religion of parkers. Rather, it sends them out as pilgrims on an unending journey.

Growth is Essential

Growth is as integral to Christian life as it is to human life. Our preacher shows his exasperation with his hearers on this. They must have been hard of hearing, he says. Though they had had ample time to mature, they were still spiritual infants, needing milk rather than solid foods.

The rebuke is reminiscent of Paul's chiding of the Corinthians, but it differs in an important way. The Corinthians *thought* they were mature, whereas these people did not even contemplate maturation. They wanted to cling fast to what they had grasped and had no intention of pressing forward. In our preacher's mind that was far more serious.

Psychologists speak today about stages of growth in faith. Faith begins with awe and wonder, with openness to learn. In an adolescent stage it solidifies and assumes more definite patterns taken over from others. If progress continues, faith advances from a kind of defensiveness toward service of others and eventually toward openness something like that of the trusting child. Mature faith is attentive to the presence of God in all of life. It is unafraid to venture forth according to the call of God, like Abraham, going to "a land he knew not whither" (11:8).

Why is growth so important? Because, the preacher observes, Christians have to have "perceptions trained to differentiate between good and evil" (5:14). It is never easy to distinguish right from wrong or to sort out life's priorities. Life confronts us with grays rather than blacks and whites. The vast range of Christian views about such issues as nuclear armaments, abortion, capital punishment, birth control, economic justice, smoking or drinking, proves that spiritual infants or dwarfs will not possess the moral skills they need to make decisions.

The Apostle Paul would concur. He prayed that the love of the Philippians, or rather God's love in them, might "grow more and more in understanding and in every perception" so that they might "have a sense of things that really matter" (Phil. 1:9-10). God's love has to sensitize our minds and condition our perceptions if we are to make the right decisions in difficult circumstances.

Here, then, is the bottom line on stagnant Christianity. It indicates that God's love is not being allowed to do what it must to effect change. The doors of hearts and minds have been pulled to and barred from the inside. Fear has taken hold and caused defenses to be erected.

According to our preacher, fear and not doubt is the antithesis of faith. That is why "boldness" is so crucial. If faith is strong, it will open us to the love of God which "casts out fear" (1 Jn. 4:18). Love will do the rest.

Pressing Forward to Maturity

Christian faith is faith directed always ahead rather than behind. "Forgetting what is behind and stretching forward toward what is ahead," Paul declares, "I press on with an eye on the goal toward the prize of the upward call of God in Christ Jesus" (Phil. 3:14). And so, too, urges the author of Hebrews.

This is not to say the past is unimportant. It is the "foundation" upon which rests the edifice of the Christian life. The problem is to keep laying down the same foundation again and again and never erecting the building itself.

We can see readily how basic these principles were: repentance, faith in God, baptism, laying on of hands, resurrection of the dead, and eternal judgment. Except for laying on of hands following baptism, these "fundamentals" have been reaffirmed and observed by virtually every group of Christians from the time of the apostle to this day.

Curiously, while observing these, some have disregarded altogether the author's main injunction to "leave the initial word about Christ and press on toward maturity" (6:1). In 1653 the General Six Principle Baptists, for instance, laid this foundation again, choosing to secure their identity around these "six principles." Clutching the past and closing their eyes to the future, they have virtually ceased to exist.

Fundamentalism proceeds in the same direction although it has laid down another set of "fundamentals" — inerrant Bible, literal virgin birth, substitutionary atonement, physical resurrection, and literal return of Jesus to earth. Concerned to guarantee universal subscription to these, it neglects to build on top of the foundation and locks Christian minds into a propositional prison which prohibits advancement toward maturity.

Hebrews presents a radically different view of faith. Faith is personal and relational. It involves illumination and tasting the gift of God and participation in the Holy Spirit and tasting the good Word of God. Once a person has experienced these, there is no turning back without awful consequences. Indeed, it would be unthinkable.

The preacher's warning here presents us with one of the most controverted statements in all of Scripture. "For it is impossible for those once enlightened . . . and falling away, again to be renewed to repentance, since they recrucify the Son of God for themselves and hold him up to public contempt" (6:4-6). Some Protestants obsessed with the question of the security of the believer have sought ways around this passage. "Once saved, always saved," they insist. "Christians can't apostatize."

We must keep in view the preacher's objective. He wanted to "scare the pants off of 'em," as it were. Some may have been toying with a return to an Essene variety of Judiasm in which they would have found legal security. Christianity was now illegal. To do that, the preacher warns, would be so drastic that such persons could not repent again, committing the "unpardonable sin."

The key issue here is repentance. To lapse from this faith, so filled with vital signs, would put us in the position of unbelievers starting all over again. Repentance is the prerequisite to faith and entrance into the covenant with God. If we had to go back to this point, we would recrucify Christ for ourselves and hold him up to public contempt again, where he has offered a sacrifice for us once for all. Notice here the preacher's emphasis on the self-centeredness of this act. Those who would lapse after receiving all of these guarantees would "recrucify *for themselves* the Son of God." Such egocentrism would preclude renewed repentance. How selfish could one be?!

An agricultural metaphor heightens the warning. Soil which absorbs the rain which falls upon it and bears good produce for those on whose account it is tilled is blessed by God. That, however, which receives the same rain and then bears thorns and thistles, obviously being unusable and thence worthy of cursing, is destined to be burned. Farmers in the congregation would readily have grasped the point. They burned off weed patches.

How are we to handle such strong words, words which have resulted sometimes in terrible agony for those who heard themselves addressed by them? John Bunyan, for example, became a manic depressive as a result of a passage from Hebrews which undermined his confidence as to whether he was among the Elect, something all Puritans wanted to know. His moods went up. They went down. He reached the point of suicide. Only those powerful words of Paul in 2 Corinthians 12:9-10 sufficed to counter these. "My grace is sufficient for you, for my power is perfected in weakness."

One thing we must make room for is exaggeration. The preacher wanted to frighten his hearers. He was pulling out all the stops. His hearers must recognize the seriousness of what some were contemplating, that it was unthinkable.

A second mitigating factor is the preacher's focus on repentance. A deed so dastardly as departure from the faith, he insists, would carry apostates beyond the pale of repentance. So long as they could repent, he seems to imply, they have hope. The only question is: How could we harden ourselves enough to the love of God that it could no longer break through? By continuous rejections, like pharaoh's, perhaps, but not by slipping a little here and there, sliding backwards or running off the main path. If we trust the author of Psalm 139, there is nowhere we can go to escape the Hound of Heaven. "If I go up into heaven, You are there. Even if I make my bed in Sheol, You are there" (Ps. 139:8).

But the most important item to keep in mind is the preacher's expression of hope for his congregation, the subject of the final paragraph. He sees some signs of salvation.

Signs of Salvation

The preacher has spotted looks of dismay on the faces of his hearers. His words have loaded them with too much weight. People have been blown away by less. So he comes with reassurance. They can have assurance not in themselves alone but rather in God's righteousness.

Question marks line the human path, and it is not surprising that we detect a questioning tone in our preacher's words. "But even if we talk like this, we are confident about you, beloved, that you will do greater things and those which pertain to salvation" (6:9). Human beings must hope, but they may fail. They are fallible.

From whence then does assurance come? Obviously from God. God is "not so unjust as to forget your work and the love which you have manifested in his name by having ministered and going on ministering to the saints" (6:10). God is a God of grace. His love pours on all. Whatever experience we have of grace and love, therefore, will come forth in like kind.

Mother Teresa of Calcutta has observed that practicing love is the key to saintliness. We cannot love God in the abstract, only through ministry to others. Her Missionaries of Charity offer "wholehearted free service to the poorest of the poor." Feeding the hungry, giving drink to the thirsty, and doing the other things cited in Matthew 25:40-46, she insists "is our only way of expressing love for God. Our love must pour on someone. The people are the means of expressing our love of God."[1]

Our preacher would agree with Rufus Jones when he warns, "To withdraw from the human press and struggle and seek only the selfish thrill of individual salvation is the way of spiritual danger."[2] But where we minister, not by compulsion but with joy and thanksgiving, we have reason to feel confident. We are seeing the signs of salvation.

We come at last, then, to the preacher's real objective. He has spoken stern and horrifying words, but he has a positive goal in mind. He wants each of his hearers to show equal eagerness to carry their hope through to the end (6:11). Christian life is like a great race. Getting to the goal with the baton in hand is what matters. For our preacher, as for Jesus, "the one who perseveres to the end will be saved" (Matt. 10:22; Mark 13:13). Those who stop or drop out along the way cannot expect to receive the prize awarded for running the race, in which we are urged on by a great cloud of witnesses and follow our pioneer, Jesus himself (Heb. 12:1).

There are models to imitiate, "those who inherit the promises through faith and patience" (6:12). Abraham is the model par excellence (v. 13), but there are lots of others. In chapter 11 the preacher will call the roll. They all exhibited a certain kind of faith and persistence, faith as belief but, much more, faith as trust and obedience and hope.

It is especially this hopeful faith which has the most relevance for trembling and fear ridden souls facing fearful circumstances. For our preacher faith and hope are virtually synonymous, for "faith is the substance of things hoped for, the proof of things not seen" (11:1). Hopeful faith stands firm in the face of the unknown and the unseen. It trusts and obeys when foundations shake and quiver. It does not give up.

The preacher's voice echoes down our corridors today. He shouts still his challenge to faithful obedience and to hopeful persistence. "Be not afraid, for God is with you," he says. "Don't stand still. Go forward."

---

[1] Mother Teresa, *The Love of Christ: Spiritual Counsels.* San Francisco: Harper & Row, 1983, p. 15.

[2] Rufus Jones, *Our Social Task and What It Demands,* pamphlet.

9

Promises, Promises!

Hebrews 6:13-20

James M. Pitts
Chaplain, Furman University, Greenville, South Carolina

Broken promises are so easily remembered. Each of us, without notice, could offer a recital of how others have disappointed us. They gave us their word that they would be with us. Together we would plan or build, dream or discover, have or hold, and now we are alone. The failure to keep promises and honor covenants has left us feeling betrayed and frustrated.

Promises, promises! "The check is in the mail." "Honey, I love you and will never leave you." "Certainly, you can count on me to be there." Verbally, we hear "I will" and "I do." The contract indicated agreement, the document with signature was properly drawn, witnessed and notarized.

Handshakes, salutes of allegiance, and kisses sealing engagements are all physically expressive ways in which we symbolically state our "yes". Thereby with that action, we pledge and commit self, money, time, loyal cooperation and faithful partnership.

We thought we understood the commitment stated verbally, in writing and by gesture. They said we were mistaken. As they walked away, they denied any accountability. The consequences were our problem.

Broken promises litter the landscape of life. In our more honest and reflective moments, we acknowledge that the problem is not only out there with "them," but also within us. We too have played word games to fog our intentions, broken vows, and simply lied, cheated and stolen.

Sensitive to the human situation, the writer of Hebrews offers encouragement by speaking of a promise that is sure and will be kept. He was addressing troubled folks whose faith was wavering. Disillusioned and yearning for the certainty of days gone by, he reminds them that God, since the beginning, has been making and keeping promises.

Their beginnings as a people were linked to Abraham. The writer recollects their patriarch as the one to whom God promised blessings. Calling Abraham out of Ur and sending him on a pilgrimage into the unknown, God initiated a unique relationship with humankind. This relationship of promise was not only to Abraham, the blessing extended on to his descendants.

Their ancestor Abraham, through the gracious promise of God, became "the father of many." He was their forebear who patiently endured and ultimately was affirmed. The fulfillment of this divine promise was not instantaneous, but an historical process. In God's good time, Abraham's trust and obedience was honored. This is evidenced by his progeny becoming a people, living as a covenant community on a faith pilgrimage to the land of promise.

Abraham's confidence was not in real estate, or humanity, or in the future, but in God. He trusted divine intention for his life and that of followers. Abraham is the example of faith and patience to be imitated by those who inherit the promise.

Oblivious to the teaching of Jesus in the Sermon on the Mount concerning refraining from oaths, the writer of Hebrews declares that God swore and he swore on himself. That is, God guaranteed and validated his promise by his very character.

The custom in mideastern society to demonstrate one was telling the truth was to impose certain curses upon oneself if lying. This convinced listeners that a testimony was true, because it was popularly believed that God would fulfill those curses if the testimony was false.

Using such a human analogy of affirmation, should God desire to offer an oath, by what higher power could he swear? There is none! So, the validation of the truth is rooted in the nature of God. His presence and his very nature guarantees it. God is his own final confirmation and endorsement. There is nothing higher, more powerful, or having greater authority than God. He offers the ultimate guarantee . . . himself!

In a world where the dynamic of change is normative, God and his way are unchanging. God does not lie. He does not deceive, mislead or misspeak. He is constantly true and trustworthy. God alone is worthy of our complete confidence. The two unchangeables in our changing world are God's promise and God's oath.

God goes all the way to demonstrate his dependability. This is evidenced again and again in our salvation-history, beginning in the creation and continuing through the faith journey of the covenant people. His trustworthiness is seen most clearly by the Christian in the life, death and resurrection of Jesus.

God continually reveals himself as creative and redemptive, suffering and triumphant love. God does not lie. God continually communicates truth through word, in flesh, and through his spirit.

Daily our homes are inundated by television scenes of old people and young children fleeing across borders. Refugees from war and famine, searching for shelter and security, clutching their meager belongings they move along roads and across fields.

What is behind is obvious. Looks of horror and fright, old scars and fresh wounds silently scream their past. Behind them is destruction and death. Ahead of these fleeing ones hopefully, is a place of hospitality offering sanctuary from the conflict. Panic stricken, these lost, lonely, helpless ones are a stampeding herd. Fleeing danger, they desperately seek a safe refuge.

What is the sign of security? In the 1960s Americans believed it was a fall-out shelter, well stocked and guarded. More recently, security has been understood to be not a hole in the ground but a cache of cash. Security is evidence in a quantity of old fashioned silver and gold. Survivalists say security is in personal firearms and well stocked pantries of food. "Political realists", as they prefer to identify themselves, say security is in a military defense with assured superiority in nuclear missiles, bombers and submarines.

In a world defined by might and power, not spirit, the writer of Hebrews uses an anachronistic metaphor in speaking of faith refugees to his audience. He symbolizes security as an anchor. "We have a sure and steadfast anchor of the soul."

A contemporary person unfamiliar with classical symbols initially finds this allusion to be obscure. An anchor in the ancient world was the symbol of hope. In the midst of a storm, an anchor is used to stabilize the position of a ship. The anchors are those heavy weights that hold the ship in place. Commonly made of iron, the flukes of the anchor dig into the bottom of the sea floor. The ropes leading from the anchors keep the vessel from drifting. Securely attached to the bottom, the anchor provides a constant in the midst of changing winds and storm tossed waves. The anchor of hope, "that sure and steadfast anchor of the soul" to which the writer alludes, is "a hope which enters into the inner shrine behind the curtain."

The Scripture writer shifts the illustration to the Holy of Holies. This is the innermost room of the Temple, where the divine presence emanated. His Jewish readers knew well the Most Holy Place, the inner shrine behind the curtain. In the heart of the Temple, the Holy of Holies was the focal place of God's presence and power.

Only once a year, on the Day of Atonement, the Temple high priest, in an elaborate ritual, would reverently enter that center of holy presence. Fogging with incense, the high priest carefully went behind the curtain and entered this shrine of divine mystery. Some believe that a rescue rope was attached to his leg and trailed back to the area where his priestly colleagues waited. Should the high priest be overwhelmed or struck down as he went in and out of that intensely sacred point of divine-human encounter, they could retrieve his body without entering the chamber. Like an anchor, he could be drawn back from the spiritual deep.

Going in and out of the Holy of Holies on that annual Day of Atonement, offering sacrifice to represent sinful people before a holy God was an awesome and threatening spiritual assignment. In our day we could compare it to a technician crawling past the containment walls and into the core of a nuclear reactor plant. As that would be emotionally draining and physically dangerous for a contemporary repairman, so it was for the priest going into spiritual ground zero. The Holy of Holies was the heart of light and life, power and potential.

No one who valued their life and had reverence for God would enter casually, but only intentionally after being chosen, carefully prepared and willing to serve as a representative between sinful humanity and a holy God. Even in this day, a pious Jew in Jerusalem is forbidden by religious law to enter the Temple Mount for fear he will transgress that powerfully sacred area. Signs on the perimeter of the temple site specifically warn and forbid such trespass. The faithful stop short, reserving a reverent distance. They go no farther than the Western or "Wailing Wall." By standing there and going no farther, they are certain not to violate the ancient site of the Holy of Holies, the innermost sanctuary of the temple.

For the ancient high priest, during the time of the temple, entering the Holy of Holies atoned for sin and prepared the way for God's promise. He traced his professional identity and tradition back to his religious ancestors. The greatest of all the priests was one called Melchizedek, a king and priest in the time of Abraham. As our spiritual forerunner, Jesus is compared to Melchizedek, a mysterious figure, a priest and king who greeted Abraham returning from battle and served him bread and wine.

Melchizedek was characterized as the ideal priest who mediated between his people and God, and was defined as the ideal king who established righteousness and peace. This pioneer and model of the perfect priest and absolute king, Melchizedek, is realized and continued in Jesus. In this grand tradition, Jesus is now the royal priest, the sinless one who offered himself as the mediator and has become our certain promise and eternal hope. For the believer, Jesus secures our access to God. He is trustworthy. His promise is sure. You can count on him!

As the child of an alcoholic parent, learning to trust has been difficult. Growing up in the midst of confusion and conflict did not encourage security and confidence. I learned early on that the only constant in such an environment was change. There was always crisis, always chaos, and the continual surprise of the unknown.

When a child's mother is an alcoholic, there is no immediate and obvious refuge. The intended nurturer and biological protector is caught up in her own sick storm of emotions. A child's dependency is just another overwhelming demand on a person drowning in a sea of substance abuse and denial. Tossed from grandiosity to disgust, over waves of chemical highs and sinking into troughs of depression, the addicted person and the family members drift out into the depths. Everyone connected, parent and child, relative and neighbor, is negatively affected and is drawn into the family trap.

With such a heritage of unreliability and instability, developing trust is difficult. For in such a setting, promises are rarely, if ever, kept. The baseline of "normal" family relationships is an unknown reference. Compensating for the deficit in missed loving and learning (for the child of an alcoholic) is a life-long recovery process.

For me, the way up and out was a sheer gift of God's grace. It came in the person of my grandmother. She offered shelter and security, loving warmth and the limits of reasonable discipline. As a youngster in the second grade, she invited me into her life and heart. No one else made such a proposal. But one offer that is true and trustworthy, especially when there were none, is more than enough.

I didn't know about refugees then. In a domestic way, however, I certainly was one. Through the word that became flesh in a grandmother, I was introduced to another. He became the significant other, who could be trusted.

Grandmother had known him most of her life. He had provided for her, even when her husband's heart failed, leaving her as a 40 year old widow with ten children to raise. He was the forerunner who went ahead on our behalf. He went all the way. He entered behind the curtain into the heart of God by way of Calvary's cross and an empty tomb. He is the sure and steadfast anchor of the soul. He is God's promise and our eternal hope.

All the saints through the ages, including my grandmother, bear witness to his name. They call him Jesus. He is God's unchanging promise. You can count on him!

10

God's Strong and Unconditional Yes To Us

Hebrews 7:1-10

Thorwald Lorenzen
Professor of Systematic Theology and Ethics
International Baptist Theological Seminary, Ruschikon, Switzerland

A Preliminary Note for the Preacher

1. This text is *difficult.* It is of central significance for Hebrews because it is part of the theological foundation which undergirds the instructions and exhortations of this letter. But "it is hard to explain" (5:11). We have no immediate access to the Jewish priesthood, to the Jewish sacrificial systems, and to the figure of Melchizedek. Also the exegetical methods employed in our text are strange to us.

This poses a dilemma for the preacher. Should we — in a sermon! — explain the strange concepts and the difficult way of argumentation so that the congregation can understand the text? The danger with this approach would be that, firstly, the sermon can easily become a lecture; secondly, the people may make intellectual assents which remain existentially meaningless; and, thirdly, we would commit the theological fallacy against which Paul warns us in Galatians 2, viz. of expecting people to adopt Jewish customs first before they could become Christians.

I would therefore propose the alternative that we try to understand the text and perceive its basic intention, and then translates the reality to which the text witnesses into our situation and into our language.

The following comments are intended to help the preacher to tune into the text. For more details a good commentary should be consulted.

2. The *situation of the people* to whom Hebrews is addressed, is marked by persecution and suffering (10:32-39). They are afraid to meet together (10:25), indeed some of them are in danger of falling "away from the living God" (3:12). It is therefore the intention of our epistle to strengthen the people's faith, to call them to obedient discipleship even when life becomes difficult, and to prepare them for hard times.

Our situation is somewhat different, but if we can think in a global perspective with its problems of hunger and poverty, the arms race and the ecology crisis, the fate of the refugees and the denial of human rights, then parallels come to mind. We may have to help the congregation to realize that human problems anywhere are also our problems.

3. Our text must be related to the *context* if we want to avoid the danger of communicating a one-sided Christology. Hebrews 4:14-10:39 proclaims Jesus Christ as the one and only true High Priest. But this does not mean that the significance of Jesus Christ is understood in terms of the Jewish priesthood and the Jewish sacrificial system. Rather the whole priestly cult is redefined in light of the Christ-event. Just as Paul proclaims Christ as the end of the law (Rom. 10:4), so Hebrews declares Christ to be the end of the religious cult.

Jesus Christ is not only superior to the prophets (1:1f.) and to angels (1:4, 2:5), but he also surpasses Abraham (7:1-10), Moses (3:1-6), and the levitical priesthood (7:15-19), and thereby eliminates the law and the cult as ways to establish and maintain a meaningful relationship to a living God. Faith is exclusively centered in Jesus Christ.

Jesus Christ can serve as the true High Priest and as "the mediator of a new covenant" (9:15) with God because he has shared in the human predicament (2:17f., 4:14-16, 5:7f.) without forsaking his faith in God (4:15); and as such he can serve as "the pioneer and perfecter of our faith" (12:2).

This emphasis on a low Christology must not be forgotten when our text begins to explain the mysterious reference to Jesus as "being designated by God a high priest after the order of Melchizedek" (5:10, compare 6:20).

4. The message of our text will become clearer when we understand the *hermeneutical principles* implied in it. *Firstly,* the author wants to preach Christ as being superior to the levitical priesthood, and as such being able to provide a firm foundation for Christian faith and hope. To do so he uses the well known story of Melchizedek. *Secondly,* the author follows the exegetical rule that if two texts contain the same concept, like Melchizedek in our case, they belong together and complement each other. In our text the author starts with Psalm 110:4 and then provides details from Genesis 14:17-24. For interpreting verse 3 it is important to know, *thirdly,* the rabbinic rule that what cannot be found in the Scripture does not exist. It is, *finally,* interesting that the author uses both scriptural (Ps. 110, Gen. 14) and non-scriptural (an early Christian poem in v. 3) texts to base his message on.

5. The following *exegetical comments* may aid a first reading of our text. Verses *1-2a* begin to interpret the reference of 5:10 and 6:20 where Jesus is designated with allusion to Psalm 110 as "a priest for ever after the order of Melchizedek" (Ps. 110:4). Reference is made to the story in Gen. 14 where Abraham fights and defeats Chedorlaomer and his allies in order to liberate his relative Lot. On his return home the battle Abraham is met by Melchizedek who — and this becomes important for our text — blesses him and "Abram gave him a tenth of everything" (Gen. 14:20).

Verse *2b* starts to conflate the story of Melchizedek with the story of Jesus Christ, the Son of God. The author interpretes Melchizedek's significance with the messianic attributes "righteousness" and "peace" (compare Is. 9:6f., 32:16f., Jer. 23:5f., 33:15, Zech. 9:9f., Mal. 4:2, Rom. 14:17, Eph. 2:14-22).

In verse *3* the author quotes a poetic or hymnic fragment which is resounded in verses 6, 8, 16, and 25. Since Melchizedek was not an Israelite, his genealogy could not be found in the Jewish Scripture. This means, according to rabbinic exegetical methods, that it does not exist. He therefore is without father and mother. The implication is that he could not be a legitimate Jewish priest, since the latter must have a spotless genealogy which proves that he is of priestly descent. The fact that Melchizedek's authority does not derive from the established Jewish historical order is further intensified by the reference to his not having "beginning of days nor end of life". Melchizedek's universal and everlasting priesthood is then likened to the Son of God. Important for the author is not that Melchizedek's priesthood lasts forever. Important is the priesthood of Jesus Christ; and the greater Melchizedek can be portrayed, the greater is the significance of Jesus. Verse 3 is the center of our text. It spells out that Melchizedek is only of importance insofar as he resembles the Son of God.

The significance of verses *4-6* becomes clear when we realize that every Israelite must pay a tithe to the levitic priesthood (Num. 18:21-24). The fact that there were no levitical priests during Abraham's time constitutes no problem to the author since they were in Abraham's loins when he met Melchizedek (v. 10). Important is only that Abraham paid his tithe to the non-Israelite priest and king Melchizedek and thereby demonstrates the superiority of Melchizedek. This superiority of Melchizedek over Abraham and the levitical priesthood is the theme of the whole section verses *4-10*. The presupposition of the argument is found in verse *7* with the implication that Abraham is inferior to Melchizedek. Since Levi was in the loins of Abraham, the whole levitical priesthood is designated as being inferior to Melchizedek (v. *9f.*). A further qualitative difference between the levitical priesthood and Melchizedek is that the latter is immortal while the former are mortal (v. *8*).

In *summary* we may say that the exegetical comments have left us with the following *theological emphases* in our text: *a*. It has become clear that the author wants to proclaim *Jesus Christ* as the one and only *true high priest*. He replaces all persons and religious institutions which have tried to provide a meaningful relationship with God. *b*. To preach Christ the author uses the story of *Melchizedek*. He does so for the following *reasons: Firstly*, Melchizedek is a *gentile*. This serves to show that God's ways to humanity are not bound to the history of Israel, or, for that manner, to any particular race or class. This is further stressed, *secondly*, by insisting that Melchizedek is *superior to Abraham* the representative of Jewish faith. *Thirdly*, Melchizedek could never qualify as a levitical priest, indeed through Abraham the whole *levitical priesthood* has paid tribute to Melchizedek and thus affirmed his superiority. Our text has, therefore, an *anti-institutional dimension*. The law and the cult have failed in establishing a meaningful relationship to God. No more sacrifices are needed (10:1-10). All that counts is following Jesus in his passion to make human life whole (13:12f.). *Fourthly*, the priesthood to which Melchizedek points does not have historical but *divine* legitimation. *c.* The *social-ethical* dimension of Christian faith is emphasized by attributing to Melchizedek the characteristics of "righteousness" and "peace".

Sermon

Introduction

a. When people experience the accepting grace of God they want to *talk* about it. When we have received some intimations of the unsearchable riches of Christ, to try to find *words* to make clear to ourselves and to others what has happened to us. How can those who have "tasted the heavenly gift" (6:4) of God's accepting love express this reality in earthly words'

This experience every Christian knows. Indeed every deliberately living person knows it. Every lover knows it. Such experiences make up the seed for poetry, for art, and for music. How can we find *words* to express, how can we find *forms* to contain the experiences which deeply effect us and shape our lives?

The author of our text is overwhelmed by the *experience of Jesus Christ*. The meaning which he sought, but failed to find in obeying the law and observing the religious cult, he found through faith in Jesus Christ. Being exposed to the story of Jesus, God himself became real to him; not as one who is far removed, not as one who can be pleased by observing the cult and obeying the law, but as the one who shares His life with our human existence and accompanies us in our earthly pilgrimage. Jesus Christ "reflects the glory of God" (1:3) in the midst of everyday life with its problems, temptations and suffering (2:18, 4:15).

b. This experience of God does not remove us from the world. It takes place in the midst of the *ambiguities of life.* We may not be persecuted for our faith as it was the case with the community to which the Epistle to the Hebrews was addressed. We may not be tempted by apostasy, as members in that church were. But do we not also experience the *world*, the *church*, and even *our lives* as *ambiguous?*

How shall we live in face of an escalating arms race which may any day issue into a nuclear big bang destroying our civilisation? How can we deal with the ecology crisis which threatens to poison the very garden which sustains us? How much longer can we take it, seeing millions of children, not to speak of their fathers and mothers, die every year because they do not have enough to eat and to drink?

And is the church not often complying with the injustices in the world. Have we not remained silent when we ought to have spoken on behalf of those who have no voice, no power, and no friends? Have we not blessed the arms which destroy human brothers and sisters? Have we not baptised a world economic order which brings wealth to ourselves but which at the same time casts millions into abject and hopeless poverty? Do we not tolerate corruption, injustice and oppression in our own midst?

Sometimes we are so overcome by the ambiguities of life that our own existence seems to disintegrate. We want to do something, but we don't know where to start. We realise the necessity for a new life style but we don't know how to go about it, because we think that we cannot live without that which we have acquired over the years. The ambiguity of the world and of the church is a real part of our own lives.

c. In such a situation the question becomes urgent: is there an anchor which can hold us in the storms of life? Is there a point of orientation which can guide us into the habor of peace and justice? Is there a message which does not simply reflect the ambiguity of the situation but which can proclaim good news to the situation? A message which is not limited to the exigencies of world and church? Which comes from the outside. A message which has a firmer foundation than what the priests of our military, economic and political establishments can proclaim to us?

God's strong and unconditional YES to us

Let us allow this text to communicate God's strong and unconditional YES into our situation of ambiguity. Our text uses the story of Melchizedek to convey to us that, if we entrust God with our lives, he can help us to deal creatively with the ambiguities of life. The figure of Melchizedek is strange to us, but the major emphases of the story may help us and challenge us for our own living.

a. Central for our text is verse 3. There Melchizedek serves as an analogy for the Son of God because "he is without father or mother or genealogy, and has neither beginning of days nor end of life". This means that God's answer to our predicament does not come out of history. God's word is spoken into our history.

Jesus Christ is called "Son of God" and "word of God" because in and with Him God has provided a model for our living which is not tainted by self-interest. He is the pioneer of a new humanity.

And is this not a message which we need to hear today? In a world where war is still an accepted means to solve human conflicts, we may discover a new dimension of life if we allow Jesus to say to us: "Love your enemies" (Matt. 5:44). In a world where our identity is shaped by what we acquire and own, Jesus could reveal to us that the key to the secrets of life is in sharing: "For whoever would save his life will lose it; and whoever loses his life for my sake and the gospel's will save it" (Mark 8:35). When Jesus says "for my sake" he invites us to share in his passion for the world. Just as he shared his life with the poor, the lame, the sick, the despised and the oppressed, so he invites us to engage our lives for those in our world who are marginalised, whose human dignity is marred. In feeding the hungry, in liberating the oppressed, in helping the tortured we are not only participating in Jesus' mission (compare Luke 4:18f.), but we are ministering to Jesus himself, for our Lord said: "as you did it to one of the least of these my brethren, you did it to me." (Matth. 25:40)

b. With this emphasis we are already at our second point: the Son of God is described as a *priest*. A priest wants to reconcile that which is estranged. He wants to bring together that which is separated. A priest wants to provide ways of meaningful relationships between humanity and God.

But how can this be done? At this point our text contains a revolutionary challenge. It announces Jesus Christ as the end of religion, if religion is understood as human strivings to please and to pacify God. Indeed, have not religious people often used the word "God" to validate their own self-interests. Our text announces that with the coming of Jesus Christ the legitimacy of the Jewish levitical priesthood is abrogated. Abraham, the representative of Jewish faith, and with him the levitical priesthood (v. 10), pay tribute to and were blessed by the gentile priest and king Melchizedek. This clearly means that the gentile Melchizedek, whose authority is not grounded in any national identity or historical tradition, is superior to Abraham and the levitical priesthood.

Why has the coming of Christ brought cultic religion to an end? Because cultic religion operates with a false understanding of God and of the human person. God is seen as a deity that can be pleased and manipulated by human acts of piety, and human persons live in the illusion that God is pleased with them when they perform these religious acts. It is an illusion because God as God can only be known in total, never in partial surrender. That is the difference between God and an idol.

With the coming of Christ the first commandment was given central relevance again: "I am the Lord your God . . . you shall have no other gods before me." (Ex. 20:2f.) When our epistle insists that Christ's sacrifice is once and for all "to save those who draw near to God through him" (7:25) it means that God has spoken his unconditional YES to us. He *is* for us. There is nothing in God which is against us. He has done and is doing all to make our life meaningful and human.

But: God is love! and as such he cannot enforce himself upon us. He pleads. He waits. He knocks at the doors of our life. But unless we will tune into his passion for the world, a passion which he has so movingly fleshed out in the life and death of his Son, we cannot know the love of God. And God's saving love is not only directed to our souls and to the church, but especially to the world! The earth is mine, says the Lord (compare Ps. 24:1). God loves and saves the world (John 3:15, 2 Cor. 5:19). With the resurrection of Jesus, God has begun to win his world back to himself. It is our privilege, and it constitutes our dignity, that we can join God's saving activity in the world. We can become fellow-workers with God. Important is not primarily or worship in the church, important is our worship of God in the world.

Just as Jesus himself spent his life with and for the poor and despised, with the sick and lonely, so we who have tasted the grace of the loving God are invited to go into the world and become representatives of God's grace there. Our epistle clarifies this critique of religion by insisting that Jesus "suffered *outside* the gate in order to sanctify the people through his own blood. *Therefore let us go forth to him outside the camp, and bear the abuse he endured.*" (13:12f. my emphasis)

Thus Christ is our priest in that with his life, death and resurrection he makes radically clear that God is for us. His grace and love become real in our lives when in obedient discipleship we join his saving passion for the world.

c. We are being told, *thirdly*, that Jesus Christ is our priest *forever* (v. 3). Melchizedek can serve as an analogy to the Son of God because "he lives" while the other heros of faith (Abraham) and of the sacrificial cult (levites) are only mortal (v. 8).

We are reminded of the promise of the risen Lord to those who in obedient discipleship will continue his mission in the world: "I am with you always, to the close of the age." (Matt. 28:20) His priesthood is not invalidated by our doubts and uncertainties. In his life Jesus has shown that God is not a God who is removed, who lives in the splendid isolation of his holiness, but that he is a passionate God. That he shares his life with our predicaments. Our epistle therefore insists that Jesus

— as the Son of God! — suffered and was tempted (2:18, 4:15), that he knew in his own life our agonies and struggles with God and with the world (5:7).

Let us say it quite emphatically: if God would not be with us in our agonies, our doubts, our temptations; if God would not be with us when we walk into the autumn of life; if God would not be passionately present in our cancer wards and our modern concentration camps, he would not be God. But it is the radiant message of the Gospel of Jesus Christ that God majors on being present when human existence seems to break apart, when our human dignity is threatened, when we suffer and die. He is present, judging those who destroy human dignity, saving those who look to God for help, and giving hope to those who struggle for liberation from oppression.

And this divine work will never finish! It is part of God's very being. It is true that he will never enforce himself upon us. But it is equally true that he will never cease knocking at the door of our lives providing ever new possibilities through which we can share in his love and passion for us and for the world (compare Rev. 3:20).

d. We have seen that Jesus Christ as Son of God described as priest because it is his concern to heal the relationship between humanity and God. This saving work will never finish. He is priest forever. It remains, *finally*, to emphasize that the priestly work of Jesus Christ is concerned with *all of life*. Not just with our souls, not just with our religious life, not just with the church, but with our bodies, with our marriages, with our business, with our politics. God has created all there is, and he wants to redeem it all.

When the German confessing church during the rise of the Hitler regime felt forced to define its own identity and mission, it said in the socalled Barmen declaration of 1934 that, on one hand, "Jesus Christ . . . is the one Word of God, whom we are to hear, whom we are to trust and obey in life and in death", and, on the other hand, that this Jesus Christ is "also God's mighty claim on our whole life . . . . We repudiate the false teaching that there are areas of our life in which we belong not to Jesus Christ but another lord, areas in which we do not need justification and sanctification through him."

This is the same emphasis which our text makes when it uses the attributes of "righteousness" and "peace" to describe Melchizedek and with him the messiah Jesus Christ (v. 2). What terrible burdens of guilt have we as Christians loaded upon ourselves when we have separated some kind of spiritual salvation from social concern, when we have given the impression that God is more concerned with the salvation of our souls than with the salvation of his world.

Today the credibility of the Christian gospel is at stake in our lives. We shall be measured by the contribution which we are prepared to make to establish justice and peace in our world. Can the church and can Christians be silent when economic and political interests threaten the survival of our civilisation? Can we, who have tasted a little of the loving grace of God, remain passive when ideological interests threaten the humane survival of the human race? Let us accept the invitation to share in the priesthood of Christ by engaging our lives for justice and peace. Thereby the life of Christ flows over into our existence and we have the glorious privilege of participating in God's mission to make human life human.

Conclusion

We want to believe in God. Even when life gets rough, when uncertainties and difficulties want to overwhelm us. Is there any meaning in the mysterious flux of history? Is there any security in the ambiguity of life? Is there life which is stronger than death? Is there love which is stronger than hate? Can there be any reconciliation in a world of self-interest, injustice and war?

Our text sounds a strong YES. This YES is grounded in the life, death and resurrection of Jesus as the Christ. Jesus Christ is described as a priest. It was indeed his passion to restore human life with God. For that passion he was prepared to die. God raised him from the dead, thereby validating Jesus' life and death, so that he could be priest forever.

How great it is to know that the reality which shaped Jesus' life can become part of our existence. He invites us to share in his priesthood. Shall we open our lives to him by sharing in God's passion for the world?

11

A Perfect and Eternal Priest

Hebrews 7:11-28

Richard A. Spencer
Professor of New Testament
Southeastern Baptist Theological Seminary, Wake Forest, North Carolina

In his rich and ingenious argument for the superiority of Jesus Christ as God's Son and appointed redeemer, the writer of *Hebrews* calls on one of the mysterious figures of the Old Testament, Melchizedek. The entire seventh chapter of *Hebrews* moves in an ever-widening spiral away from this figure to the Son of God who supercedes this legendary priest-king. In making his point that Christ is superior to Melchizedek, the author argues this way. Melchizedek, the priest-king to whom father Abraham paid tithe of his spoils, is like God's Son in that he is eternal (vv. 1-3); his priesthood is superior to that of Abraham's descendants the Levites (vv. 4-10); because the levitical priests could not secure lasting perfection for the people it was necessary for another priesthood to be instituted (vv. 11-14); this new priesthood sets aside the old law and replaces it with a better means to God (vv. 15-19); the unique surety of the effectiveness of this new priesthood is that God himself has sworn it (vv. 20-22); there is only one priest in this new order, not many as in the levitical priesthood (vv. 23-25); this new priest is God's own appointed Son exalted in the heavens.

Much of *Hebrews* seems strange to us, and no aspect of it more so than the priestly imagery of chapter 7. In our ecclesiastical and liturgical traditions the sacrifice of animals for us by a religious leader is completely foreign. In fact, it is heresy for us to allow a priest to serve as mediator between people and

God. We emphasize the priesthood of every believer. Moreover, the religious leaders to whom we do extend leadership roles are "called" to the task by God's invitation. They do not inherit their office.

And so this text with its priests and priestly lines, its law and sacrifices, oaths and covenants addresses us as a word from another place and time. But beyond those strange images there is a word from God for us as well.

As we listen to the text we must first try to hear the word of God as it came to those ancient Jewish Christians in ways they could understand. This means we must appreciate the Temple, priests, the law and God's covenant. Now if we were sharing our faith with an unbeliever we would hardly set for ourselves the task of first teaching him or her all about the Temple, priests, law, and covenant. But such matters were all-important to the original readers of *Hebrews*.

The people who first read *Hebrews* were much different from us. They had been reared thinking of the Temple in Jerusalem as God's dwelling place. It was there, in that place, that humans could come to God. That was God's plan. Moreover, God had ordained that only a special family or tribe could serve in the Temple as mediators between God and people. The class whose job it was to oversee the cultus and provide religious continuity and stability was that of the priests. These men had been entrusted with Israel's soul as well as with sacred traditions. It was their charge to serve as Israel's representatives to keep the covenant relationship whole.

The religious "constitution" which justified and prescribed this priestly role was the Torah or law. To many a common person of the first century the law was only a burden to endure or to ignore. Those who understood the law in its best sense thought of God's law as his revelation of what he required of his people. The law outlined social and religious patterns for responsible living. In that sense the law was an expression of God's loving concern for his people. It was an unparalleled expression of love that God would conjoin himself so freely to a humble slave people. Thus, the law was God's loving self-communication.

The law was undergirded by a relationship between God and his people, an agreement, a covenant. The binding agreement between God and his people involved privilege and responsibility, the privilege of God's continuing presence with his covenant people and the responsibility of that people to live up to his demands. It was relationship at its most wholesome and mature state. As the centuries passed this covenant did not grow weak with age but rather gained strength. Among the truly religious Jews the covenant was an overarching reality of life, as constant as the circuit of the sun and as binding as gravity. It was the arena within which all other relationships of life were defined. The covenant guaranteed a protective and responsible relationship for the people. To be sure, by the first century A.D. many corrupting influences had marred the surface of Judaism. But the sacrificial and priestly cultus still dominated the life of observing Jews.

And yet, as magnificent as were these witnesses to God's concern for his people, there was a very basic insufficiency about them. They were bound in time; they were means to a temporal end. The Temple — as stable a factor in Judaism as it was — was the *third* temple built on the same site. And it was destroyed by the Romans in 70 A.D. The intricately-developed genealogical and ecclesiastical system for perpetuating the priestly lines and orders of service would pass away with the Temple. And even before the destruction of the Temple, there was a brittle historical network that guaranteed priestly succession. Many priests were required to keep the system working. The law had to be developed and expanded by the rabbis over the centuries so as to make it meaningful to their particular needs. As a result, from 10 commandments there developed 613 commandments. The law, too, suffered change. The covenant which bound God and his people would itself be changed. Jeremiah had prophecied its replacement with a new covenant (Jer. 31:31-34). Both the early Christians and the Dead Sea Sect seized on this promise and described their respective communities as the people of the new covenant.

Everything basic to Jewish faith, then, was temporal, finite, transitory. Everything was subject to change or replacement. The writer of *Hebrews* capitalized on this factor to make his point about the pre-eminence of Christ. Christ's purification is not one in an endless repetition of purifications. His priestly work brings completeness, perfection before God (v. 11). His priesthood is not inherited but appointed eternally, by the Father. That means the law (what God reveals as his expectations) is replaced. The new covenant (v. 22) is God-given and as certain as God's own oath to himself. This one priest, Jesus, makes a once-for-all offering which is eternally valid.

When we view the message of *Hebrews* like this, we begin to press beyond the particulars of this word to first century Jewish Christians and to hear the eternal word of God for us today. This text tells us

- that Jesus is unique in nature and office
- that his sacrifice is once-for-all
- that Jesus alone can give us God's forgiveness and grace.

The purpose of *Hebrews* is to make a strong statement on the pre-eminence of Christ. In these verses the writer shows the pre-eminence of Christ over all rules, rituals, and religious systems. He moves from the immanent to the transcendent, from time to eternity, by speaking of the mysterious Melchizedek of legend and patriarchal narrative. But Melchizedek is only a transition figure. The writer has his eyes fixed on Jesus all the time. It is a word about Jesus, God's Son, that burns within this writer, not a word about Melchizedek.

Jesus is unique in his nature and his office. While the priests of ancient Israel were holy men, they were men at best. They were mortal, fallible, and limited to their human frame. Jesus, on the other hand, is the effulgence of the Father, bearing the very stamp of God's own nature (1:3). When we see Jesus we see God revealed perfectly, clearly. Our high priest is not sinful but sinless, not short-lived but eternal, not one of us but one from God for us. He is God's Son, and thereby pre-eminent in his nature. His work as high priest is pre-eminent over all other priestly functions. He does not have to repeat the sacrificial act. His own sacrificial act of offering himself for us is the final sacrifice. It cannot be superceded or canceled. It is good for all time and all people. His ready and everlasting access to God on our behalf is guaranteed by God's own promise made to himself. Until God decides to lie to himself and break his own oath to himself (which will never happen) we *have* the perfect, sinless high priest to see us through to the Father. That wonderful priest is none other than Jesus.

Jesus' sacrifice is once-for-all. Jesus is uniquely qualified to be our mediator. He can represent us in our weakness and failure because in the days of his flesh he was tested and tempted as we are and can sympathize with us (4:14-5:10). At the same time, in his perfection, purity and holiness he can represent God. It is Jesus alone who is qualified to do the reconciling work of bringing God and people together. Two distinctives of his sacrifice force us to pay closer attention to his unique work. First, what he offers is not the life of a goat, bull, sheep, or dove but *his own* life. This priest who would give us new life does so by laying down his own life. No other sacrifice could measure up to his. Secondly, because of this insuperable sacrifice, it cannot be repeated. It is sufficient and effective forever. One of the main differences between Protestants and Catholics can be seen in the crosses they use. In the Catholic Church the crucifix has Christ affixed forever. That is their way of affirming the eternal effectiveness of the cross. Protestants feel that such an interpretation, coupled with the Catholic transformation of wafer and wine into the body and blood of Jesus in the mass, miss the point of the once-and-for all nature of his sacrifice. So, in Protestant churches, for the most part, the cross is empty. The sacrifice, having been made, is done forever. What the text means is that Christ's sacrifice is unique and insuperable.

Jesus alone can give us God's forgiveness and grace. In our time of secularism and laissez-faire thinking, we see an erosion of emphasis on the absolute uniqueness of our Lord. There are many fine and admirable philosophies and systems of self-help about. But nothing compares to Jesus. We can find no higher plateau from which to peer into the cosmic depths than in Jesus. We can have no clearer image of the nature and demand of God than we find in Jesus. We can know no more certain forgiveness of sin than in the Carpenter from Nazareth. We can find no more able mediator between us and the Almighty God than Jesus. We can experience no greater gift of love than in the self-giving sacrifice of our great high priest Jesus.

The world has had its series of great men and women, great social and political leaders, great philosophies, great teachings, great books, and great religious systems, many of which have lifted and inspired the masses for a while. But they all fall short of the incomparable excellence of the God-appointed Son, our perfect and eternal priest before God.

12

Waiting for the Van

Hebrews 8:1-13

Thomas H. Conley

Senior Minister, Northside Drive Baptist Church, Atlanta, Georgia

The car choked and sputtered its way into the entrance of the local auto dealership and cut off. Jay Hardy let it coast until it was well within the bay doors.

"Morning, Dr. Hardy."

"Morning, Ralph."

"Trouble again, Doctor?"

"Yep. I hope it's warranty stuff this time. See what you can do with it. By the way Ralph, I'll need a lift to church."

"Well, Doctor, the van just left. Ought to be another out in about twenty minutes or so. Please have a cup of our complimentary coffee and wait in the lounge." He smiled. Their complimentary coffee was well-known throughout the city.

Jay chuckled. "Pour some of that complimentary coffee into my car. That ought to unclog whatever ails it."

"Sure, sure," laughed Ralph. "I know what you think of our coffee."

Jay Hardy pulled open the door to the lounge and headed for the coffee pot and the stack of styrofoam cups on the table. The television was on, and "Good Morning America's" David Hartman was interviewing some fellow who was about to do a daredevil stunt of some kind. Jay didn't catch the trick to be done.

He retrieved his coffee and sat down two seats from a man who was intently reading *Sports Illustrated.* An attractive woman across from Jay sat with her fur coat wrapped tightly around her. She was not doing anything specific. A glance here and there, an occasional nod toward the television, almost too low to be heard. An elderly woman with her hair pulled back in a bun sat at the end of the room. She was totally immersed in a thin ragged-edge book. Her demeanor was one of confidence and she looked self-possessed, even serene. Jay had not seen that for a long time.

Hardy had just opened his book and begun to read when the door swung open. He recalled later that at that very instant he felt as if an invasion were occurring. The door was ripped open and a large man swaggered in. His tousled hair accented his red face. He had on a black suit with a bright red tie and the shirt collar ends curled up unceremoniously. He had a huge stomach that protruded over his low-slung belt. He carried a large black book in his arms.

"What a day it is out there. Rainy, wet and cold. But I never judge a day by its weather. The Lord has still made a beautiful day." He pounced into the chair by the woman in the fur coat. She scooted to the opposite edge of the chair and gave him a look that said: "How *could* you sit next to me?" The man with the *Sports Illustrated* went deeper into the magazine. The woman with the bun never looked up. She was completely enamored with her reading. And while no one gave a verbal response to the man's bluster, Jay could tell everyone in the room had negative body language.

Jay looked hard at the black book. It appeared to be one of those floppy reference Bibles, but surely not. He went back to his reading and then he heard the man, in lower tones, address the woman in the fur coat.

"You know the Lord can just take a messy day like today and fill it with blessing." Jay looked up. The woman smiled and looked toward the television. The man went on, moving to the edge of his chair.

"Of course not everyone knows the joy of Jesus as personal Savior. And that. That makes the difference. But then I imagine you're a Christian, aren't you?" He had leaned over close to the woman and had taken away the edge that her "scoot" had margined for her.

"Yes," she said weakly. "I am, thank you."

"Well, praise the Lord!" His rough-hewn voice filled the small waiting room.

Jay had been pastor of The First Baptist Church in his city for over a dozen years. He hadn't seen or heard such a brazen "witness" since his college days. He was determined, however, not to get involved. He followed the man's example two seats over. He went deeper into his book.

"Yes, sir, being a Christian is the most wonderful thing in the world. I can't tell you how meaningful it makes life, don't you think?" he asked the woman next to him. "By the way, my name is Billy Bluff."

She nodded and Jay, who had looked up again, saw a red blush creeping up the side her neck in blotchy patches.

"And what do you think being a Christian means, sir?" The voice had come from the woman with her hair in a bun. She was turning a page of her frayed book but had never even looked up.

Jay wished she had not done that. He consciously scooted down in the chair and lost at least two inches off his six-two frame.

Billy Bluff moved closer to the edge of his chair, his huge frame hanging on the front like a balanced tight-rope walker.

"It means belief in Jesus Christ."

"What else?" she asked.

What *was* she doing? Why didn't she concur and let the fellow hush!

"It means believing in the Bible as the inerrant word of God." He shook the big black Bible in his hand and held it up. All his life Jay Hardy had fought stereotypic responses to people and ideas. He considered himself to be an open and progressive pastor and he had always tried to respond to persons as persons and not labels. He felt that he was looking flush into the face of a stereotype. But it was real, the fellow was there and his ace, pressed on the too-tight shirt collar, was getting more red with each exchange.

"What else does it mean?" the woman asked. She still had not looked up.

"It means believing in the Virgin Birth of Jesus and his deity. And it means believing in the substitutionary atonement, the blood bank of Calvary. It means believing in the bodily resurrection of Jesus from the dead and the imminent second coming of Jesus to judge the quick and the dead."

Billy sat back as if to say, "Well, I've told it all." The woman who still had not looked up went on, much to the dismay of Jay Hardy.

"And can I be a good Christian and not believe all those things?"

"Why . . . why . . . no, I don't think so, why would you *want* to be a Christian without believing those?"

"Because my understanding of the faith says that the heart of it is a relationship with the Christ and not in a list of creedal statements." Jay could not believe he, Jay Hardy, had said that. After all those vows of silence he made at the beginning of this encounter. He had spoken clearly and with authority. For the first time the woman with the bun looked up and smiled.

"You mean you think you can be a Christian and not believe what I've just said?" asked Billy, edging more toward the end of the chair.

"Sure you can be. As a matter of fact I have been for most of my life and I'm fifty-three now."

Billy Bluff began to thumb through his floppy Bible.

"But the Bible says, even in the *Old Testament*, that the *Word* of God will endure forever."

"I believe that," said Jay, "but I think God is constantly renewing his word . . ."

"Or *her* word," said the woman with the bun.

"Or *her* word," reiterated Jay. "And God is constantly making a new covenant. There's a passage in that Bible of yours which says that God will 'draw up a new covenant with the people of Israel and with the people of Judah' (Hebrews 8:8). And the writer goes on to say about this new covenant: 'I will put my laws in their minds and write them on their hearts' (8:10). Now that to me means God has established a new way to reveal who he, or she, is. That spells relationship, *internal* relationship to me and moves me away from a list of creedal statements and closer to a person."

Jay finished and Billy Bluff rose to his feet and then sat down just as quickly.

"Now wait a minute. You mean to tell me that you think you can be Christian just with a personal relationship with Jesus Christ?"

"Yes." Both Jay and the woman with the bun answered at the same time.

"And you mean," he said, getting redder in the face all the time, "that you don't believe those fundamental things I mentioned before?"

"The point is, my friend," spoke Jay, "that whether I believe some of those or not, I have the freedom in my relationship with Christ and within that new covenant to process experientially whatever it is about Christ that I may come to believe. And I have the right and freedom to come to very different conclusions than you and still be just as Christian as you are. It's the principles of Jesus Christ in our hearts and minds that determine our beliefs, not statements written on a piece of paper."

The woman with the bun joined in. "Those creeds and doctrines written down are helpful but they are never to be used to judge my experience with the Christ. They are the frames that carry the pictures of how others have found Christ to be. But that's all . . . at least for me."

Billy Bluff looked from Jay to the woman with the bun. "Are you two together?"

"Well, no," said Jay. "At least we didn't come together. Although there seems to be some theological affinity here."

At the use of "theological affinity" the man reading *Sports Illustrated* lifted his eyebrows and looked askance at Jay as if to ask, "Who in heaven's name *are* you?"

"So," said Billy, "You two" — and he waggled his finger back and forth between Jay and his compatriot at the end of the room — "you two don't affirm the great fundamentals of the faith, huh?"

The woman in the fur coat, sensing the confrontation was getting hotter went for the coffee pot and the man reading by Jay traded his *Sports Illustrated* for a *National Geographic*. Jay thought in that fleeting moment how much easier it would be just to look at the pictures and listen.

"My friend," said Jay, "it is not that I don't necessarily believe or disbelieve your list. What I'm saying is you can be a fine Christian without affirming any or all of those. I remember the words of Judge Learned Hand: 'The spirit of liberty is the spirit that is not too sure it is right.' "

Billy jumped up and came across at Jay: "Then you aren't *sure* you're right?"

"I'm sure enough to live by it, but not sure enough to say that you have to."

"But the Bible is the Word of God and it says . . . ." Jay interrupted.

"The Bible *is* the Word, but so is Jesus the Christ. *He*, as *the* Word, has given the law, the prophets, the writings, a whole new dimension. As I see it, the relationship with *the* Word, Jesus, is the most crucial part of faith."

Billy was flushed and by this time prancing up and down the small room. Jay looked at his watch. "Where *is* that van?" he asked himself. Billy had been searching through his Bible.

"Now you quoted Hebrews 8 a minute ago. I've got it now." He read intently to himself a minute and then squeezed in between Jay and the man reading *National Geographic*. The fellow threw down the magazine and virtually bolted across the room to the coffee pot and then took a seat in a "neutral corner."

Billy had found him a passage. "Look here. Read this." And he began to read Hebrews 8:6 in a loud voice.

> But now, Jesus has been given priestly work which is superior to theirs, just as the covenant which he arranged between God and his people is a better one, because it is based on promises of better things (TEV).

"How can you believe in Jesus as priest if you don't believe in the Virgin Birth and the substitutionary atonement?" Billy asked, his jaw jutting forward rebelliously.

"He didn't say he believed in or disbelieved in any of those, Mr. Bluff; I believe the gentleman simply said that his personal relationship with Christ was the heart of his faith, not his affirmation of doctrinal statements and creeds regardless of how 'right' they may be." The woman in the bun was still reading and she spoke, turning the page of her book, never looking up.

Billy Bluff turned to Jay Hardy. "Is that what you believe?"

"Exactly. It's not that statements and doctrinal concepts are unimportant, but if I put them first they become my priest and my creed becomes the hub of my faith instead of the Christ. Not only that, I tend to lose perspective and think I have to defend the creed and I put the relationship with Christ on the back burner, so to speak. Then, too, I lose the spirit of the Christ and become defender of the faith. I tend to feel, Mr. Bluff, that neither God nor his faith needs much defending."

"Priorities, Mr. Bluff, priorities," spoke the woman with the bun. "The relationship defines the creed. The creed does not define the relationship. The relationship rests upon freedom of experience. The creed has its own vested interests and demands that experience reflect those interests. Is that what you're saying Dr. Hardy?"

Jay was astonished. How did she know his name? And those words were very familiar. He stammered out: "Yes ... uh ... yes, that's ... uh, right. Exactly."

"O.K. folks, the van's here. All aboard." It was wonderful to hear Ralph's voice.

"Thank God," breathed the man whose stint with the magazines he gladly surrendered. He and the woman in the fur both made for the door and arrived at the same time almost getting stuck.

Billy Bluff was right behind them. Jay waited for the woman with the bun.

"How did you know who I was?"

"Oh," she said with a twinkle in her eye, "I make it a point to know whom I can trust in a community. I'm Ruth Johnson. I teach philosophy at City College, but I've known about you for a long time. I'm a member of another church in the city but I've heard you speak and I must say," she turned over the book she had been reading, "I like your last book, *The Priesthood of Christ*, very much." She smiled a broad, warm smile and looked pleased with herself. Jay suddenly knew why those words she had quoted moments before were so familiar.

The van roared off. Billy Bluff sat quietly with his big Bible. The magazine reader and the woman in her fur had sat down next to each other and were talking quietly. Jay and Ruth sat together. Had anyone told him that he would have spent this incredible half an hour in a car dealer's waiting room he would have said, "No way!"

His new friend, Ruth, began to talk as they rounded the corner into the new day

"By the way, Dr. Hardy. Since you were quoting *Hebrews* in our conversation with Mr. Bluff, I'm sure you remember the last sentence, don't you?

> By speaking of a new covenant, he has pronounced the first one old; and anything that is growing old and ageing will shortly disappear (8:13 NEB).

Mr. Bluff is surely one of God's children. But I kept thinking that the last line of *Hebrews* 8 spoke to his approach. It seems to be 'growing old and will shortly disappear.' Or at least, I think it should."

Jay nodded affirmatively. Ruth went on. "By the way, Dr. Hardy, have you read the new book by . . . . . "

Unbelievable!

13

The Only Sacrifice that Matters

Hebrews 10:1-18

David Matthews
Senior Minister, First Baptist Church, Greenville, South Carolina

One of the most memorable opening lines to a sermon I ever heard was from Dr. George Kelsey in seminary chapel. I had never seen or heard him before. I trembled at the deep voice that came rolling out of that great black face. He said, "There is a fundamental wrongness in the world."

He was right, of course. We have know it nearly all our lives, in our hearts if not in our minds. All people of all times and places have had some sense of it in their depths. In this creation that is our home, there is something fundamentally wrong. And whatever it is, it is inside each one of us, too.

Usually we are not very good at diagnosing our own problems, however. There is the story about the man who was suffering from hay fever. He went to the library to read about his ailment in a medical encyclopedia. As he thumbed through the big book, he became intrigued with some of the many diseases listed there. Suddenly he froze with fear. As he read the symptoms for typhoid fever, he realized he had had it for months. He came across something called St. Vitus' Dance, and, to his surprise, found that he had those symptoms, too. Greatly distured he began reading the encyclopedia alphabetically. He found he had Bright's disease in a mild form and cholera with severe complications. He concluded he had had diphtheria from birth. Later he said, "When I went into the library, I was a healthy man. When I came out, I was a physical wreck."

Whatever may be the many diagnoses or misdiagnoses, whatever may be our other problems, the fundamental problem, of course, is sin. The clear message of our Bible, from beginning to end, is that sin has alienated us from God. Because of our disobedience we are estranged from the One who is both the source and the meaning of our lives.

The twin facts about our human condition, profoundly stated in Genesis and assumed everywhere else in the Bible, are, first, that we are made for fellowship with God, and, second, that we are not what we are meant to be. If we have eyes to see, this is confirmed everywhere we look. F. W. Dillistone says:

> . . . in whatever direction we look — in the realms of race, of colour, of class, of culture, of community, of personal relationship, of psychological adjustment — one question overshadows all others. It is the question of Alienation, or Estrangement. (*The Christian Understanding of Atonement*, Philadelphia: Westminster Press, 1968, p. 2.)

No one talks much about sin, says Dillistone, but everyone talks about alienation, from the secular historians to the secular psychoanalysts. In literature and art, especially in the twentieth century, humans are seen as alienated from themselves, from the past, from other people, from nature. It can be a pretty negative picture.

So, the terrible reality of sin, by whatever name it is called, is sensed in the depths of the human soul. With it, there is the feeling that something must be done about it. What can we do?

Offerings for Sin

Sacrifice has a long history in our world. Often it is a grim history. It was not uncommon for ancient people to sacrifice their first-born children, so strong was the compulsion to make things right with the higher powers. The lengthy and sordid list of inhuman practices to appease divine beings gives you some idea of how those divine beings were conceived.

In our Bible, from the earliest times until the destruction of the second temple in 70 A.D., sacrifices were a central part of the religious life. There were many kinds of sacrifices and offerings, and they did not all have the same motivation or significance. But, basically, they were an attempt to do something about *the problem.* They were a way of making something right with God.

We've come a long way. We don't do such things. We don't make sacrifices, offerings for sin. Don't we?

Surely more of what we do than we know is motivated by the partly conscious, partly sub-conscious belief that God's favor has to be won. How much of the average person's church attendance, gifts of money, acts of kindness, and expressions of piety are attempts to please or appease God? God only knows.

There is something of the Elder Brother from Jesus' famous parable in all of us. We think if we are good boys and girls we deserve good treatment. Sometimes we are good boys and girls in order to get good treatment.

The writer of Hebrews would have us understand that our offerings for sin, whatever they are, do not solve the problem. Israel had sensed this fundamental need to be put right with God. But Israel failed to understand how this happens, and sought justification in the law, in general, and in the sacrificial system, in particular.

However, says Hebrews, "the law has but a shadow of the good things to come instead of the true form of these realities" (10:1). And, "it is impossible that the blood of bulls and goats should take away sins" (10:4).

Here is the devastating conclusion of the matter. It is not just that the sacrificial system of ancient Israel was inadequate. It is that none of our offerings for sin, and no offering that we could make, can put us right with God. The breach is fundamental. It is eternally serious. If you have cancer, taking two aspirin every four hours just will not provide a cure.

When you are the problem, help just may have to come from beyond you. The New Testament is sure: our offerings may have value for many other things, but for the forgiveness of sin they are useless. We cannot save ourselves.

The Lamb of God

In my Pastor's Discovery Class for older children, we talk about sin being what separates us from God. We talk about how this separation is the root of all other problems. We talk about how helpless we are to do anything about it, despite all our capacities to do good things, create beautiful things, and gain great power. I ask, "If *we* can do nothing to overcome this separation from God, what is our only hope?" They always see. "That God will do something about it."

The anonymous writer of Hebrews writes that when Christ came into the world he said:

> Sacrifices and offerings thou hast not desired, but a body hast thou prepared for me; in burnt offerings and sin offerings thou has taken no pleasure. Then I said, "Lo, I have come to do thy will, O God," and it is written of me in the roll of the book. (10:5-7)

This is a quote from Psalm 40:6-8, but put in the mouth of Jesus. This, Christ himself would have us know, is the meaning of his coming. The sacrificial system is nothing. He has come to live out the will of God . . . bodily. And the offering of his very life provides for the salvation of sinners (10:8-10). By the accomplishment of the will of God "we have been sanctified through the offering of the body of Jesus Christ once for all" (10:10).

Here is the meaning of grace. What God demands, he provides. He does for us what we cannot do for ourselves. He himself makes the only sacrifice that matters.

Do you remember what John the Baptist said when he saw Jesus approaching? He cried: "Behold, the Lamb of God, who takes away the sin of the world!" (John 1:29). Do you recall the words of Acts 8:32, taken from Isaiah 53:7? "As a sheep led to the slaughter or a lamb before its shearer is dumb, so he opens not his mouth." And there are the two verses in 1 Peter 1: "You know that you were ransomed from the futile ways inherited from your fathers, not with perishable things such as silver or gold, but with the precious blood of Christ, like that of a lamb without blemish or spot" (vs. 18-19). In the book of Revelation there are nearly thirty references to Jesus Christ as the Lamb of God.

What God demands, he provides. This is the only sacrifice that matters.

There is great grace, too, in that what was done in Christ was done once for all. It does not have to be done over and over again. To use his own words, "It is finished."

Hebrews says:

> But when Christ had offered for all time a single sacrifice for sins, he sat down at the right hand of God, then to wait until his enemies should be made a stool for his feet. For by a single offering he has perfected for all time those who are sanctified. (10:12-14).

This is contrasted with the Jewish priest of old, who stood every day at his work, "offering repeatedly the same sacrifices, which can never take away sins" (10:11). Or, we would say, it could be contrasted to contemporary people who strain daily to prove themselves by attaining success (our culture's chief virtue), or who grit their teeth in their efforts at perfection, or who otherwise engage in fruitless efforts at self-justification.

What Christ has done has been *done*, completed. That he sits at the right hand of God waiting for his enemies to be made his footstool simply means that he has won the final victory. One day this will be manifested for all to see. In the end, suffering love triumphs.

So, the cross represents the only sacrifice that matters. On it love fulfilled itself by emptying itself. On this cross the only one who could save us became one of us, experienced our kind of alienated dying, and defeated death by accepting it. On this cross God joined our dying, and through a sealed and guarded tomb opened a way through death to life.

A way for whom? For all. For whosoever will. I learned the words as a child. They mean more now.

> "Whosoever will, whosoever will,
> Send the proclamation over vale and hill;
> Tis the loving Father calls the wanderer home;
> Whosoever will may come."

Behold, the Lamb of God who taketh away the sin of the world.

Offerings of Love

Are we therefore completely off the hook? If Christ's death on the cross is the only sacrifice that matters, are we therefore free to forget the matter?

Some in the early church thought so. The deed is done, they said. Salvation is ours. The work of redemption is finished. We may live as we please. If there is grace for sin, then let sin abound that grace may abound the more.

It is not what God had in mind. It is not what God intended when he provided the only sacrifice that matters. Listen to the writer of Hebrews:

> This is the covenant that I will make with them after those days, says the Lord: I will put my laws on their hearts, and write them on their minds, . . . I will remember their sins and their misdeeds no more (10:16-17).

God had in mind a new people, a people who would be his own people. God intended a people who would live forgiven, and who, in that joy, would be obedient to his holy will.

He did not make us free so that we might return to all of the bondage from which we have been delivered. He made us free that we might fulfill his high purpose for us. Surely out of gratitude for what he had done we would live in obedience to what he knows is best for us. Given such unthinkable love, how could we do otherwise?

Perhaps you will remember the lovely story of Cagular, a political resister in the days of Cyrus, who lived on the southern border of that great empire. This chieftain consistently defeated the small detachments of Cyrus' army that were sent to subdue him. Finally, the emperor sent his whole army and the chieftain Cagular was captured.

He and his family were brought to the capital for trial and execution. On the appointed day Cagular and his family stood in the judgment hall before Cyrus.

Cyrus was impressed by this handsome and fearless man, his noble wife, and his two beautiful children. Finally, Cyrus said, "What would you do, Cagular, if I should spare your life?" "Your majesty," came the reply, "if you spared my life I would return to my home and remain your obedient servant as long as I live."

Cyrus asked, "What would you do if I should spare the lives of your children?" "Your majesty, if you spared the lives of my children I would gather my scattered horde, place your banner over them, and lead them to victory on many fields of battle."

Cyrus asked, "And what would you do if I spared the life of your wife?" "Your majesty, if you spared the life of my wife, I would die for you."

So moved was the emperor that he freed them all and returned Cagular to his province to act as governor thereof. On the way home, Cagular asked his wife, "Did you notice the marble at the entrance of the palace, the different colors and the figures so perfectly formed?" "No," she said, "I did not notice the marble." "Did you notice the tapestry on the wall of the corridor outside the great hall? It was magnificent!" "No," she said, "I did not notice the tapestry." "Surely you noticed the emperor's throne. It seemed to have been carved from one lump of gold." "No," she said, "I did not notice the throne."

Cagular asked, "Did you see nothing?" She answered, "On the way in I was too full of fear to see, and on the way out I beheld only the face of the man who said he would die for me."

Look again at the cross. See how much you are loved.

When there is forgiveness of sin, when the only sacrifice that matters has been made, there are no more offerings for sin. But there should be offerings of love. Should there not?

14

The Fourth Exhortation

Hebrews 10:19-39

Dale Moody
Retired Professor of Christian Theology
The Southern Baptist Theological Seminary, Louisville, Kentucky

Of the five exhortations about the possibility of apostasy in Hebrews, the fourth is perhaps most neglected and rejected, yet it is the least ambiguous in meaning.

This fourth exhortation has three paragraphs. The first may be called: The New and Living Way — Hebrews 10:19-25. If, as I believe, Hebrews was written to Christian believers under persecution, either in Rome or Jerusalem, the siege of Jerusalem between 66-70 offers the best background of understanding. The crucial question in whether the destruction of the Temple would mark the departure of God's presence from Jerusalem.

The belief was that the death of Jesus was the sacrifice that was once-for-all and made unnecessary the repetition of the day of Atonement, the holiest day in the year in Judaism. Jesus has become "the new and living way" into the sanctuary in which he is both high priest and sacrifice "over the house of God." The earthly sanctuary may pass away, but the heavenly sanctuary now fully revealed in Jesus will never pass away.

This fourth exhortation introduced with faith, hope and love is really a preview to the last three chapters of Hebrews with the greatest chapter on faith in the Bible (11), one of the most important chapters on hope (12) and concluding admonitions introduced with a call to brotherly love (13).

Each of the so called theological virtues is introduced with "let us." Once when being interpreted in another language the congregation was told that I was about to speak on "rabbit food." Not exactly, but it is definitely "soul food" for the faithful.

We are to "draw near with a true heart in full assurance of faith, with our hearts sprinkled clean from an evil conscience and our bodies washed with pure water" (10:22). Some of the most important words for faithfulness appear. The "true heart" expresses the positive side of genuine trust in a Hebrew way, while "evil conscience" is the negative side described in a Greek way. Heart and conscience are at other places key words in Hebrews.

A most instructive term is "full assurance" (plerophoria), a much stronger term than assurance. With "full assurance" believers become less likely to go back into unbelief. It is the lack of "full assurance" that is so dangerous. To deny this danger for ourselves and others is deceptive talk.

The second call is to "hold fast the confession of our hope without wavering, for he who promised is faithful." The faithfulness of God is ever true, but it is our unfaithfulness that may be in danger. A faithful saying says (2 Tim. 2:11-13):

> If we have died with him,
> we shall also live with him;
> if we endure with him,
> we shall also reign with him;
> if we deny him,
> he will also deny us;
> if we are faithless,
> he remains faithful—
> for he cannot deny himself.

Those who use this saying to support the belief that a believer can later become an unbeliever and an atheist and still be eternally secure in his salvation lead people astray. See W. O. Vaught, *Believe, Plus Nothing*, 1983, p. 28 for such teaching.

The third call is to "consider how to stir up one another to love and good works." These words are written in the week of my father's death, January 7, 1985. I have written and spoken millions and millions of words to stir up people to love, but my Dad had a fifth grade education and was a man of few words. I am left with the question if his life of love and good works, mentioned in so many ways, was not more acceptable to God.

Time after time I remember the cold mornings on a small farm and ranch when he would rise early to stir up the coals and put on more wood for the comfort of his family.

One morning I saw these words in the Dallas Morning News that was thrown regularly on our porch.

> I like my friends like I like my fires,
> Open and ruddy to the seasoned core,
> Sweet fibered and hickory hearted,
> The sort you can warm your life by.

The two old fireplaces at each end of the old two-storied house picture the prayer that was created in my heart among the simple pioneer people at home and in little one-room churches in those days. I have long believed the most important thing done by the church is "meeting" or as Hebrews 10:25 says: "Not neglecting to meet together, as is the habit of some, but encouraging one another, and all the more as you see the day drawing near." We may try to do things through the churches in a bigger way, but we will never be "church" in a better way.

Apostasy as Wilful Sin (Hebrews 10:16-31).

I trust that the reader has already read chapter 55 of my book *The Word of Truth* (Eerdmans, 1981) in which I discuss this biblical doctrine in a larger context.

In the introduction to that chapter I explained that I was using the word apostasy as it was used in Hebrews 3:12, where the Greek for "departing" or "falling away" is *apostenai*.

I also explained how Hebrews is the major New Testament writing on apostasy, although I quote from 26 of the 27 New Testament books in support of the view expressed in the five long warnings against the danger of apostasy (2:1-4; 3:7-4:13; 6:4-6; 10:26-31 and 12:14-17).

I have chosen to expand part of the fourth warning which is Hebrews 10:26-31. Remember that I believe the supreme authority for all faith and practice is the Scripture. It is to be put above all human tradition whether they be creeds, confessions or popular cliches. I am completely committed to Article I of the *Abstract of Principles* of The Southern Baptist Theological Seminary where I have been a teacher for the last 37 years. Article I says:

> The Scriptures of the Old and New Testament were given by inspiration of God, and are the only sufficient, certain and authoritative rules of all saving knowledge, faith and obedience.

At the beginning of Article XVIII the *Abstract of Principles* says:

> God alone is Lord of the conscience; and He hath left it free from the doctrines and commandments of men which are in anything contrary to His Word, or not contained in it.

To these principles of Scripture and conscience I am completely committed.

There are three points in Hebrews 10:26.

1. **If We Go on Sinning Deliberately.**

What is wilful or deliberate sin? What does the literal translation of the first line in Hebrews 10:26 mean when it says: "If we keep on sinning deliberately or wilfully"?

The Old Testament background to this passage is Numbers 15:30. If you begin reading at Numbers 15:22 you will note that sins done out of human weakness and ignorance can be forgiven. These are called errors and sins committed unwittingly. The worst of human sins, even adultery and murder, can be forgiven.

There is only one sin for which there is no sacrifice and no forgiveness. That is called *presumptuous* sin or sin committed with a high hand (Numbers 15:30).

The best recent statement on the meaning of wilful sin by a Baptist writer is in a book called *Hebrews* (Tyndale, 1976), dedicated to W. A. Criswell and written by a past President of the Southern Baptist Convention, James T. Draper, Jr. His excellent summary says:

> Here is someone who has been saved and yet maliciously, wilfully, deliberately plots to disobey God, to rebel against God.

> This does not refer to an accidental sin. It is not merely an isolated act of sin or lust or passion. This text refers to careful, premeditated, deliberate sin against God by a believer. It shows a Christian who acts knowing that his deed is against God, against his will, against his purpose. And in spite of it all, he shakes his fist in the face of God and says, "Leave me alone. I will do as I please." It is wilful premeditated rebellion (pp. 278f).

Excellent statement! Excellent statement!

2. **After Receiving the Knowledge of the Truth.**

In the interest of brevity I will again make reference to the excellent statement on the meaning of knowledge *(epignosis)* in the book of *Hebrews* by James T. Draper, Jr. Herschel H. Hobbs argued the same in his *Studies in Hebrews* (Convention Press, 1954) and his *Hebrews* (Broadman Press, 1971), first published as *How to Follow Jesus.* I am very happy to agree with these two outstanding pastors on these first two points.

James T. Draper, Jr. must have used a Greek lexicon or a good concordance when he listed 2 Peter 1:2; 1 Timothy 2:4; 2 Timothy 3:7; Ephesians 1:17, 18; 4:13; and Romans 10:2 to demonstrate the point that *(epignosis)* (knowledge) really means "full knowledge" as H. H. Hobbs argued many years earlier.

Strangely enough James T. Draper, Jr. did not use the most powerful passage on *(epignosis)* (full knowledge). That passage is 2 Peter 2:20-22. The noun is used once in 2:20 and the verb is used twice in 2:21.

Now read carefully and prayerfully 2 Peter 2:20, R.S.V.

Let me put two questions. First, how can they get "tangled again in them and overcome" if they were not first tangled, then got untangled, then "tangled again in them and overcome"? Second, how can the "last state" be worse than the "first state" in which they were entangled in "the defilements of the world" and a "last state" when they went back to the "defilements of the world"? It is clear that they went back to the state before believing.

Now look at 2 Peter 2:21 where the verb for knowledge *(epignosko)* is used twice:

Another question! Would it not be necessary to go some distance on "the way of righteousness" before they could turn back from the holy commandments delivered to them? You can't turn back before you have gone forward.

This great passage on the apostasy of those who have *full knowledge* of the truth is sealed with Proverbs 26:11 in 1 Peter 2:22.

3. **There No Longer Remains a Sacrifice for Sins.**

Those who accept the first two points made by Hobbs and Draper run into great difficulty in their defense of tradition over Scripture when they come to this third point in Hebrews 10:26.

Some argue that the sacrifice of Christ was for *sin*, not for *sins* (see H. H. Hobbs), but this will not hold. This is the tenth time in ten chapters that Hebrews has made reference to *sins*. In Hebrews 10:12, just above Hebrews 10:26, are these words (R.S.V.): "But when Christ had offered for all time a single sacrifice for *sins*, he sat down on the right hand of God." Do as Draper did on full knowledge *(epignosis)* and look up all the references to *sin* and *sins* in Hebrews and you will discover that any distinction between Christ's sacrifice for *sins* and for *sin* is without foundation in fact.

Still others try to get out of the corner into which they have painted themselves by appealing to the word "judgment" *(krisis)*. Judgment *(krisis)* in Hebrews 10:27 has the same meaning as judgment in Hebrews 9:27f which says:

> And just as it is appointed men to die once and after that comes judgment *(krisis)*, so Christ having been offered once to bear the *sins* of many, will appear a second time not to deal with *sin* but to save those who are eagerly waiting for him.

If I had the opportunity to preach a second sermon it would surely be on Hebrews 9:23-29, but I am not given that much time.

Hebrews 10:27 is not speaking of the judgment seat of Christ where rewards are received or withheld from the saved. Had he had in mind the judgment seat of Christ, he would have used the Greek word *(bema)* (cf. 2 Cor. 5:10).

There is a third phrase that is often neglected by many, but it is the clincher for what follows. The phrase "fury of fire that will consume the adversaries" comes from Isaiah 26:11 where Isaiah 26:10 calls the "adversaries" or the "enemies" of God "the wicked." Then Isaiah 26:14 described them as those who will have no part in the resurrection to life. There is no question that Hebrews 10:27 describes the destiny of the damned.

The reason for this destiny of the damned is described in great detail by the contrast between the punishment *(timoria)* of sinners in the Old Covenant of the Old Testament and the punishment *(timoria)* of apostate sinners in the New Covenant of the New Testament.

Hebrews 10:28 quotes Deuteronomy 32:35-36 as follows: "A man who has violated the law of Moses dies without mercy at the testimony of two or three witnesses."

Those who have no sacrifice for their sins and are therefore damned have three witnesses against them.

First, they have stomped the Son of God under their feet (10:29). Do you really believe a person can stomp the Son of God under his feet and still be saved? Do you?

Second, the apostates have treated as unholy the blood of the new covenant with which they were sanctified. The use of the singular in Hebrews 10:29 brings the sin to each one of us. Do you really believe that a person can treat the blood of Christ as profane or unholy and still be saved? Do you?

Under the old covenant, as Hebrews 9:22 says, almost everything is purified with blood, and without the shedding of blood there is no forgiveness of *sins.* The blood of Christ is the basis for the forgiveness of all sins of all times. No person has ever been saved and no person will ever be saved who has profaned the blood of Christ.

The third witness against apostates says they have "outraged the Spirit of grace" (10:29). The nearest thing to this in the Old Testament is the grieving of God's Holy Spirit in Isaiah 63:10 which says:

> But they rebelled
>   and grieved his Holy Spirit;
> therefore he turned to be their enemy,
>   and himself fought against them.

This is quoted in part in Ephesians 4:30.

Let me ask again. Do you really believe that a person can come before God at the final judgment with no sacrifice for his sins and still be saved? Do you really believe one can stomp the Son of God under his feet, treat as unholy the blood of Christ of the New Covenant with which he was sanctified, and outrage "the Spirit of grace" and come before God at the final judgment as a "saved" person? Do you?

The answer to all these questions is found in the conclusion of Hebrews 10:30f. "For we know him who said, 'Vengeance is mine, I will repay.' "

The Perseverance of the Saints

Preaching on the previous paragraph (10:26-31) precipitated a crisis in my teaching career of forty years, so it has been pondered carefully for any evidence of error. None has been found and not one person has made an effort to refute my exegesis. This following paragraph (10:32-39) has only strengthened my sense of exegetical integrity.

The behavior here described is definitely that of believers who are under pressure to become unbelievers again. The "after receiving the knowledge of the truth" (10:26) is now "after you were enlightened" (10:32). The old cliche that says they had illumination *without* salvation is as impossible here as in the previous reference (6:4). Illumination "belongs to salvation" (6:9). See also the exposition of 6:4-6.

The perseverance of the saints (10:32-34) is introduced with a vivid picture of *the persecution* of the saints. It is possible that a passage in the *Annals* of Tacitus (15:44) has reference to the same ordeal of suffering and loss of property. After Nero burned Rome, July 19, A.D. 64 he looked for a scapegoat among the Christians:

> Accordingly, an arrest was made of all who pleaded guilty; then, upon their information, an immense multitude was convicted, not so much of the crime of firing the city, as if hatred against mankind. Mockery of every sort was added to their deaths. Covered with the skins of beasts, they were torn by dogs and perished, or were nailed to crosses, or were doomed to the flames and burnt, to serve as nightly illumination, when daylight had expired. *The Complete Works of Tacitus*, New York: The Modern Library, 1942, p. 381.

Tacitus clearly did not think the Christians were guilty and speaks only of the "glut of one man's cruelty."

The Roman destiny has been challenged since the studies of Qumran have accumulated. Moses Stuart, as far back as 1828, argued for a Palestinian origin and destiny of the letter. George Wesley Buchanan, *The Anchor Bible*, vol. 36, *To the Hebrews* (Garden City, New York: Doubleday and Co., 1981), pp. 255-267.

A Palestinian Christian (Barnabas?, Acts 4:36) may have written from Caesarea to former Essenes now Christians in Jerusalem during the Jewish War of 66-73 A.D., described in such detail in Josephus' *Jewish War.* In any case the contents indicate a crisis in the community in which many were tempted to escape from suffering by apostasy (2:1-4; 3:7-4:11; 6:1-29; 10:19-39; 12:1-29).

The appeal to Habakkuk 2:3-4 as the call for perseverance (10:35-39) does suggest Essene background. A commentary on Habakkuk was found at Qumran. By the translation of *hypomone* as perseverance in the NIV (10:36, 12:1) a distorted term has been given a more biblical meaning by putting the emphasis on the future continuation of the Christian life rather than the mere commencement in the past. That is why salvation always has a future reference in Hebrews (1:14; 2:10; 5:9; 6:9; 9:28).

15

The Characteristics of Faith

Hebrews 11:1-40

T. C. Smith
Emeritus Professor of Religion
Furman University, Greenville, Sorth Carolina

If we polled Christians who read their Bibles frequently and asked them what chapter in the *Epistle to the Hebrews* stands as the greatest and best known to them, I imagine the majority would select the eleventh chapter. Perhaps their choice of this chapter came because it speaks of heroes of Old Testament days. However, few would venture to ask why the author deemed it necessary to present this hall of fame. If we study this section in the context of the whole epistle, we can fully understand why the author inserted this roll call of the faithful.

In the last part of chapter 10 the readers are summoned to reflect on the good old days when their faith was strong and stable. They had endured a tremendous amount of suffering. They were insulted and received physical injury. They visited those of their number who were imprisoned, and they accepted with joy the confiscation of their property. After the first barrage of persecution subsided, some members of the congregation lost their ability to remain firm and steadfast in the faith. They were shrinking back into apostasy and were in danger of defecting. Realizing the seriousness of the situation, the author brought to their attention a description of faith with illustrious examples from the time of Abel to the Maccabean martyrs. He hoped that his readers might perceive that they were not alone in their struggle. Others faced the same obstacles in the past, and their boldness and stability made them victorious. They were models paraded before the readers to stimulate them to stand firm in the present crisis. As these heroes of the past were an inspiration to the reader of this epistle, in like manner they speak to us today.

The author of Hebrews begins by giving us a short description of faith. He did not intend for us to use it as a definition because faith can never be fully defined. For him faith is the way by which invisible realities become real for people. No one should ever consider faith as inferior knowledge since it is not based on empirical evidence. In fact it is the proper mode of knowledge in relation to unseen realities. Faith is complete reliance on God by trusting in his purpose, power, wisdom, and mercy. It is the movement of finite life toward the infinite promise of God. There is a depth about faith which we in our conventional piety have failed to comprehend. Unless God matters ultimately, he does not matter at all. There is something about faith that demands all. It is not just one more frill to add to the other attachments of life. It is an attachment without which all other attachments are meaningless. If faith is genuine, it is all.

The chief qualities of faith demonstrated by these noble examples of the past are three. They possessed a faith characterized by adventure, endurance, and influence. *Faith gives us a sense of adventure.* Several years ago one of the oil companies had a slogan which was displayed in many magazines. The slogan was "Mankind fares as the pioneer dares." Every time humanity has struck its tents and pressed forward, some person with courage has become a pioneer striking against the shackles of current opinion. From Abraham to the Apostle Paul, from Joan of Arc to Lincoln, from the founders of our country to those who walk in space, there was always present the confidence that the impossible was possible. Throughout all generations improvements in all areas of life have been initiated by those who had a faith of adventure.

It would have been much easier for Abraham to remain in Ur of the Chaldees, living in secure and familiar ways and holding fast to the beliefs and practices that had stood the test of time. However, he and his family went with his father Terah to Haran. There he responded to the call of God to become a bedouin and move to a land of promise. Abraham went out under sealed orders. He ventured into the unknown with no guarantee of a safe return. He did not know where he was going, but he trusted God. According to Genesis Abraham's objective was the land of Canaan, but the author of Hebrews says that he was looking for a city with foundations whose builder and maker was God. The great discoveries of the 15th and 16th centuries expanded the horizons of western civilization because a sailor from Genoa, Italy had a dream. He believed that if he sailed west across the Atlantic he could touch the shores of India. He responded to this conviction by seeking aid for his voyage from Italy, Portugal, and England. The rank and file of people laughed at him and said that he was insane. Scientists and businessmen believed the journey was possible but gave no financial support for the venture. Finally, he was able to persuade Queen Isabella of Spain. She sold her jewels and fitted out three ships because she trusted the conviction of Christopher Columbus. While Columbus was mistaken in his destination, we are forever indebted to him for his faith of adventure because apart from him we would not live in this land today. In the field of science we have had countless scientists who contested the current opinions of their day with an undaunted faith in their theories. They responded to their convictions by performing experiment after experiment in laboratories. Finally, their theories became facts. Because of their diligence and convictions they have contributed to the well-being of people throughout the world.

In the area of Christian missions all progress has been attributed to those who had a faith of adventure. In the day of the Apostle Paul the Jewish Christians refused to accept a Gentile into the Christian fellowship unless the convert was circumcised and first of all became a Jew. Paul resisted this opinion because he believed a person came into a right relationship with God by faith in Christ apart from the observance of the Mosaic law. He not only held this conviction but responded by proclaiming the freedom of the Gospel to the Gentile world. Because of the conviction and response of Paul we are followers of Christ today.

In the last decade of the 18th century some Christians in England were saying that when God chose to convert the heathen he would do it in his own time and in his own way. Others contended that Jesus' command to his disciples to teach all nations was not obligatory on all succeeding ministers. A few believed that nothing could be done before another Pentecost. A shoemaker, called into the ministry and sent out by the church at Olney, did not share these opinions. In 1792 he preached a sermon in Nottingham with these two divisions: "Expect great things from God" and "Attempt great things for God." William Carey responded to his conviction by going to India as a missionary with little support from his own Baptist denomination and none from the established church. Because of the faith and response of Carey we witnessed the beginning of a brilliant chapter in the history of modern missions. We can take comfort in knowledge that there are missionaries today in every land under the sun.

It is easy for us today to glory in the bravery of the heroes of the past who had a faith of adventure. We honor them and sing songs of praise to them because of their dedication to the task of releasing humanity from the bondage of tradition. However, we do not have the same courage to challenge current opinion of our own era so that changes may occur. We too need a faith of adventure.

A second characteristic of faith displayed by the heroes in the eleventh chapter of Hebrews was endurance. Moses gave up wealth and position of royalty to endure the humiliation of Israelite slaves with a hope of leading them out of Egyptian bondage. He endured as seeing him who was invisible. Rahab, the harlot of Jericho, risked the hostility of her people when she changed her loyalty to tradition and threw in her lot with the people of God. When Abraham went to the land of Canaan, he lived there as a foreigner. He knew this was not his true home. He lived in tents, a temporary and unsettled way of life. He did this because he did not expect much of this life. When Noah was building his ark in anticipation of the great flood to come, perhaps he suffered the taunts, sneers, jeers, and mockery of his neighbors as they asked him, "Where's the rain?" In addition to the known individuals in the hall of fame who had patience in the midst of adverse circumstances, the author of Hebrews extolled the nameless for their steadfastness. Some were tortured, imprisoned, stoned, killed by the sword, cut up by saws. Others were destitute, afflicted, ill-treated. Still others wandered over deserts and mountains, and lived in dens and caves. All these did not throw in the towel. They had an enduring faith.

When we read our New Testament carefully, we will discover that "endurance" as a noun or "endure" as a verb occur more frequently than the vast majority of our other theological words. The preponderance of the usage of endurance and endure in the vocabulary of the early Christian community ought to make us aware of their importance. Yet we are prone to overlook them or place them on the fringe of Christian faith. Not so for the author of Hebrews. He saw that members of his congregation or another congregation had lost their patience and endurance. They were on the verge of capitulating and turning their backs on God. This is why he set forth models of the past who remained steadfast in the presence of hardships, uncertainties, and suffering. Indeed they could profit from their example. Never before in the history of the Christian movement has there been such an all-out effort to proclaim the good news of Christ to those who have not confessed faith in him. We sponsor evangelistic conferences, evangelistic campaigns, mission projects, seminars on lay witnessing, door-to-door visitation, television evangelism, and religious tract distribution. The Southern Baptist Convention adopted several years ago the slogan "Bold Mission Thrust." Tied up with the slogan is the goal to proclaim Christ to the whole world by the year 2000.

All of these campaigns, projects, and programs have good and well meaning objectives, but they are limited in scope. They stress witnessing for Christ. They are interested in telling people how to become Christians. They emphasize the initial step of faith, but we have to move on to another question: Will this experience last? Is it just a "flash in the pan" affair? Along with faith in Christ that brings us into a right relationship with God, we need an enduring faith. As the Apostle Paul put it in Romans 1:17, our right relationship with God begins with faith and continues through faith in Christ. The Christian experience is tied to faith from beginning to end. Those who depend more on self-confidence than confidence in God or engage in chest-thumping heroics based upon emotion and not reason are sitting ducks to be shot down when life gets rough.

For some, endurance assumes a passive role in life. This was the answer of the Stoics. When they encountered suffering, shattered hopes, and insults, they could grin and bear them. They could take adversity on the chin. Endurance in the Christian faith is of a different breed. It is not patience that bows its head and allows all things to descend on it in a passive sort of way. It is not bearing things and accepting God's will with dumb resignation. Endurance is a quality that keeps people on their feet with their faces to the wind and a song of praise on their lips. Can we say with Job under the adverse circumstances of life, "The Lord gives and the Lord takes away, blessed by the name of the Lord?" Can we say with the banished Duke in Shakespeare's play *As You Like It:*

> "Sweet are the uses of adversity,
> Which like a toad, ugly and venomous
> Wears yet a precious jewel in her head.
> And this our life exempt from public haunt,
> Finds tongues in trees, sermons in stones,
> Books in running brooks, good in everything,
> I would not change it."

After our first enthusiasm has worn off, we need an enduring faith to keep us. In the Little Apocalypse of Mark 13, Jesus speaks of wars, rumors of wars, nation against nation, famine, trouble, and sorrows. This is the kind of world we live in. It is no easy reading fiction that tells about living happily ever after. However, Jesus went on to remind us that the person who endures to the end shall be saved. Above the doubt and unbelief of the world, above the world of dark uncertainties is the faith of endurance that causes us to rebound from the terrific impacts of life, the blows of misfortune, and the heavy strains of the odds against us.

A third quality of faith is influence. Influence is that which we pour out of ourselves into someone else by what we feel, think, do, or say. We never see it, nor do we hear it. Yet, consciously or unconsciously, every moment of our lives we exert an influence for good or bad. Influence moves and acts in ways incapable of being explained. It is silent, magnetic, and pervasive. Our influence is not simply confined and limited to ourselves nor to our own arena of action. It extends to others and will reach succeeding generations. We live and die and the good and bad live after us. What is done is done and will blend with the boundless everworking universe either for good or evil, openly or secretly.

Abraham interpreted God's will to mean that he was to sacrifice his son Isaac. He journeyed to Moriah in obedience to what he thought was God's intention. The trial in the case of Abraham was not so much a conflict between natural affection toward his son and obedience to God. It was a conflict of apparent inconsistency concerning God's previous revelation to him. Abraham had received the promise that through Isaac his descendants would be innumerable as the stars in the heavens and the sand on the seashore. How could the promise remain in effect, if he sacrificed his son? Isaac represented all the influence Abraham had. Did God want him to terminate it with a sacrificial knife? The inflexible faith of Abraam was rewarded. The life of his son was spared, and the promise of his influence remained firm and sure. Abraham, as well as the other heroes of the Old Testament, died in faith without witnessing their descendants mounting to the proportions in the promise of God. There was partial realization, but the fullness they saw from afar, and they saluted the prospects. They all knew that their influence was contributing to the formation of a society which had foundations constructed by the creator of the universe and the maker of humanity. Many of us today repeatedly face those moments when we honestly believe that nothing will ever be achieved by our proclamation of the Gospel or living the Christian way of life. We throw up our hands and say, "I am just a drop in the bucket. I am only one out of many. What sort of change can I make in life against such heavy odds?" This faulty thinking comes because we believe that influence has to be measured by huge numbers of people we affect. If we measure our influence by numbers, we have already won the victory. There are enough Christians in the world to change the world overnight. Our problem is a lack of commitment to Christ. Someone has said, "There is not enough difference between those on the inside of the church and those on the outside to strike up a contrast."

The community of faith that Jesus founded numbered only a handful of disciples. The boldest of them denied him. One betrayed him. All the others fled when he was captured in the Garden of Gethsemane. They were poor, uneducated, and hopeless. These disciples did not have a single synagogue which they could claim as their own. If they spoke their own language, Aramaic, listeners could quickly recognize it as a mongrel dialect. If they tried to speak the Koine Greek, the world language of the day, it was a miserable patois. So weak and feeble were these disciples, it would have been foolish partiality to predict for them even a limited existence as a Galilean sect. But what happened? This small group, limited in every way, turned the world upside down. No, we do not need numbers. We need people fully dedicated to the truth of God revealed in Jesus Christ.

Not only are we misled by numbers in thinking that we do not exert an influence, but we are impatient and desire immediate results. If our thoughts, our messages, and our efforts are not immediately appreciated, we give up and say, "What is the use?" Yet, we must realize that the good we do today may not have its full effect upon life for years to come. We do not live just for today. We live for the future. The heroes of faith do not disappear at the end of chapter eleven. They come before us again at the beginning of chapter twelve. The author gives us the imagery of a stadium in which the ex-champions of faith sit as spectators cheering the present competitors who are engaged in a gigantic relay race. The athletic event is not a hundred or two hundred meters dash. It is a long-distance run. The participants must be stripped for action to have any chance of winning the race. They must lay aside every encumbrance, the nature of which is explained by the additional phrase "sin which readily clings to us." Since it is a long-distance run, the competitors are not asked to display a final spurt to the finishing line but to run with endurance the race that lies before them.

In this spectacular contest in which we are also engaged there comes the appeal not to focus attention on our own progress nor on the multitude of the faithful in the stadium. We appreciate the interest and cheers of these invisible onlookers who have handed down the baton of faith to us. Our eyes must be fixed on Jesus who stands at the finishing line. He is the source, guide, and perfecter of faith. He is the exemplar of faith from start to finish.

16

Developing Christian Endurance

Hebrews 12:1-11

Robert C. Mulkey
Pastor, First Baptist Church, Deland, Florida

There is a long hill near the house where I lived as a boy. One day I had a friend visiting me who suggested that we run down that long hill together. We started down the deserted country road, and half way down I developed a side stitch and sat down. My friend ran on to the bottom of the hill and back up to where I sat. It was a humiliating experience. Later I learned that the way you become able to run a distance is by running regularly and by pushing on through your tiredness and pain each time you run. The day I ran all the way down that hill and all the way back up with relative ease was a day of quiet victory for me.

No one can run with endurance without some work to build up that endurance. The writer of The Letter to the Hebrews tells his readers how they can build up their endurance for the long race that lies ahead of them.

Hebrews is addressed to Christian people who were anxious and discouraged. They were helplessly watching storm clouds of persecution build up and darken the horizon. Some of their members were already forsaking their assemblies, turning back from their commitment, and refusing to bear the reproach that came with being a Christian. The Roman emperor Nero was beginning to impose his order. No deaths had yet come, but both the writer of this long sermon and his readers knew that the worst was just ahead. He was giving them hope to endure a harsh period of persecution.

How would these discouraged and distressed Christians get themselves ready for the race that lay before them? The writer says "Fortify yourselves with these truths. Tape these to your bathroom mirrors and keep yourselves reminded every day."

> We are surrounded by a cloud of witnesses, martyrs whose sufferings it is our privilege to share (11:39-12:1). We have Jesus as our example of faithful endurance (12:2). We may face hostility but it will never compare to the rejection Jesus suffered (12:3-4). We are looking toward a time when God will show us that our sufferings have helped to make us His children (12:7-11).

The cloud of witnesses includes those of the "by faith" roll call of chapter eleven. We are never alone in our struggle to be faithful to Christ because of all those heroes of the faith who watch as if they surrounded us like spectators in an athletic arena. We are the runners. We have been in training. We have stripped off all the heavy clothes that would slow us down. We have fought against our own sinfulness. That has been a battle in itself because our sin "dogs our feet" (Phillips). All of that self-discipline will enable us to endure a long, hard race. But the real stamina will come from remembering who is in the stands.

It is easy to see how this kind of inspiration works in the mind and spirit of a modern-day runner. The Boston Marathon has become an amazing phenomenon with hundreds of runners enduring the twenty-six miles because they have been inspired in their training by heroes of running like Bill Rogers and Jim Fixx. And suppose you are running a race and know that all the great runners, living and dead, are watching you. It does something to you just to think about their presence, knowing that they have paid the price and have done what you are trying to do.

The message for us twentieth-century Christians (we need all the hope and encouragement we can get) is that we should surround ourselves with a cloud of witnesses. Know who your heroes of the faith are. Learn all you can about them. Think often of the price they paid and of how they endured.

As I look at the media produced heroes and heroines of today, I realize that it is not simply a good idea for Christians to develop their own lists of heroes, it is absolutely mandatory. We need them to displace the glossy, transitory heroes whose pictures and stories bombard our minds from TV screens and magazine covers. Ask yourself: "Who are my cloud of witnesses?" Say to yourself, "I can choose them with the guidance of the Holy Spirit, and I can choose to be inspired by them."

I would choose for my cloud of witnesses some whom I came to know as a child through Bible stories and others whom I have known and read about as an adult. I am inviting them all to surround me: Joseph, David, Peter, Martin Luther, John Wesley, David Livingstone, Harry Emerson Fosdick, E. Stanley Jones, Clarence Jordan, Martin Luther King, Jr., Mother Teresa. There are others whose names are not well known, such as my pastor when I was a teenager and one of my church members who is currently facing the ravages of cancer with great courage.

Remembering that we are surrounded by a great cloud of witnesses builds up our endurance. We don't have to stop at remembering that they are there. We can also choose them and invite them to surround us. We can read and think about their stories. Knowing that they have paid the price to run the race ahead of us, we are encouraged to run it too — with endurance.

The writer of Hebrews presents Jesus in a way that is unique in the New Testament. Not only is Jesus the object of our faith, he is also our best example of a man of faith. Jesus is quoted as saying, "I will put my trust in God" (2:13). The writer says that he was "tempted as we are, yet without sinning" (4:15), and that "he learned obedience through what he suffered" (5:8). Jesus really has experienced what it is like to live by faith and not by sight. He has had to learn through suffering. That sounds like our struggle. He is truly a brother who has walked in our shoes. Yet, he is not just another hero. He is way out ahead, and he is at the source of our faith.

It is interesting how many variations there are on the words describing Jesus in 12:2. You can hardly find two translations that are alike. He is "author and finisher of our faith" (KJV). He is the one "on whom our faith depends from beginning to end" (TEV). He is "pioneer and perfector" (RSV), "source and goal" (Phillips), "founder and guiding spirit" (Cottonpatch). He is "the one who leads us in our faith and brings it to perfection" (JB). All of these translations indicate that Jesus is our example of endurance. He endured the cross despite all of the shame it brought him in the eyes of his people. In doing that he became our best example; now he is seated at the right hand of God. He is our fixed point of reference like the North Star for a navigator. The writer describes his eternal place in this way: "Jesus Christ, the same yesterday, today, and forever" (13:8).

We can never understand all that it means for Jesus Christ to be unchanging. But it means at least this: his life and death are always our number one example of what it means to "run the race with endurance." God has certified that by raising him from the dead and by making his example to be above all other examples. That will always be true. He does not change.

Recently, I watched an installment of David Attenborough's *The Living Planet* television series. He was high up in the Himalayan Mountains. Holding up a fossilized sea animal, he asked, "How did these fossils get here?" After a series of illustrations of how the earth's crust is shifting and changing, evidenced by volcanoes and lava flows, Attenborough answered his question with a convincing theory. The land mass which is now India once lay separated from the Asian continent. As it moved in and connected itself to the larger land mass, it pushed the area that had been seashore up into mountains that are now the Himalayas. We tend to think of mountains as unchanging. In fact they change drastically over time. Nothing that is perceived through our five senses is unchanging. Everything is changing. But Jesus Christ, toward whom we look as the goal of our faith, is "the same yesterday, today, and forever." There is no other totally trustworthy guide or goal for your life.

In his attempt to prepare us to face the long hard race with endurance, the writer of Hebrews asks us to remember our cloud of witnesses, to look to Jesus as our highest example of endurance. Then he tells us that whatever hostility we face is minuscule beside the rejection Jesus suffered (12:3-4). What he says of his first century audience is true of us: ". . . you have not yet resisted to the point of shedding your blood." Yet we know plenty of struggles against sin.

Hardly a month goes by that I do not receive a brochure from some organization offering to teach me how to handle my stress. It seems to me that most of my stress comes from the church. Most Christians face their worst opposition not from worldly and godless sinners but from Christian sinners. Recently a burned-out church member said to me, "I hope there is no church in heaven." I understood what he was feeling. There are many Christians in the world today, however, who are facing the rejection of their society and even of their own families. When Hebrews was written, Christians were experiencing the hostility of Jewish religious leaders and the growing official persecution of the Roman government. Soon many would die in the Neronian persecution. Their suffering would be a participation in Christ's sufferings and in the sufferings of those heroes of the faith in chapter eleven. The way for persecuted Christians to keep from being discouraged is to remember that Jesus put up with so much hatred.

Who can compare his sufferings with the sufferings of Jesus? There are many who have suffered more physically, but he endured the utter rejection of those whom he truly loved. Jesus went to the cross bearing more than we can imagine, because the worst kind of hurt is being rejected by someone you love and seek to give your best. David Wilkerson, of Teen Challenge, told in a sermon of a Pentecostal preacher who brought his sons to him for help. He begged his sons to enter the Teen Challenge program to get them free of their drug addiction. Then he poured out the story of how hard it had been to accept the fact that his two sons, brought up in the church, had gotten hooked on drugs and then had begun to sell them. According to Wilkerson, as the man broke down in sobs, his two sons got up from their chairs, looked at their father with cold disgust, walked past him, and disappeared out the door. It was that kind of hatred that Jesus faced. He was despised and rejected by the people he loved as only he could love. We may face the hostility and even the hatred of others because of our faith in Christ, but whatever we encounter, Jesus suffered more rejection than any of us will ever suffer.

We develop endurance as Christians by remembering that we are surrounded by a cloud of witnesses, by looking to Jesus as our example and remembering his sufferings, and by looking ahead toward the time when God will show us that our sufferings have helped to make us a part of his family.

The writer of Hebrews asks us to choose carefully the attitude we will take toward the struggles we face. He says there are two ways to look at our suffering that will help us to endure. First, we can accept suffering as discipline which God uses to shape us and which proves that we are his children. Second, we can accept suffering as discipline that will form in us a spirit of peace and righteousness.

Parents who love their children discipline them. If we experience the disciplining hand of God in our lives, that shows we are his children. I admire people who relate their sufferings to what God is trying to teach them. They don't blame God. They simply look for the ways in which he is using the suffering as a productive discipline in their lives. For example, I walked into the hospital room of a man in his early thirties who was suffering from a rare disease of the digestive system. He had been receiving nothing by mouth, not even water, for three weeks. All his nutriments were being fed to him intravenously in hopes that his digestive system could get some rest and fight off the disease. He had been living through bouts like that for seven years. As we talked, he said to me, "I'm praying that God will heal me. Meanwhile I'm going to learn something new every day and not let myself get stagnant and depressed. That wouldn't help anybody and it would make me sicker than I am now." From all I could tell, he was succeeding in learning and in staying up emotionally. He was, and is, radiating joy in the midst of a difficult physical struggle.

Peace and righteousness are the fruits of discipline. Running the long, pain-filled race with endurance leads to joy. Jesus did not escape paying the price of discipline. Neither can we if we follow him. The writer of Hebrews indicates that Jesus ran the very same race we must run. We can look ahead and see him encouraging and coaching us to run with endurance. We can see that he expects more out of us than we have been giving. If we keep our eyes on him, we will finish the race. There is always the temptation to look at some people and think, "They are so far ahead of me I'll never make it. I can't be the kind of Christian they are." There is the temptation to look at some who seem to be falling behind us and think, "I am so far ahead of them, I can take life easy." Comparing ourselves with others tempts us to become discouraged on the one hand, or to develop a prideful sense of superiority on the other. That is why Jesus is the one to whom we should look for strength to run with endurance. Knowing that he is looking on and that his spirit is in our cloud of witnesses will give us the endurance we need.

Arturo Toscanini received a posthumous award from the Academy of Recording Arts and Sciences in 1984. In a National Public Radio discussion of his great power as a conductor, an admirer said that Toscanini made musicians do their best work and brought out of them what they were really capable of doing. How did he do it? The admirer told of a conversation between two musicians following a performance conducted by Toscanini. One of them said, "He had his eyes fixed right on me during the entire performance." The other musician replied, "That's not true. He kept his eyes on me the whole time."

Christian endurance comes from knowing that you are surrounded by a great cloud of witnesses. It comes from looking to Jesus as your example of faith. It comes from knowing what Jesus suffered for you. It comes from knowing that your sufferings are being used as God's good discipline. Christian endurance comes from knowing that Jesus, "the founder and guiding spirit of our way of life," has his eyes fixed right on you for the whole performance.

17

Spiritual Health and Proper Worship

Hebrews 12:12-29

Cecil P. Staton, Jr.
Graduate Student Regent's Park College
University of Oxford, Oxford, England

The book of Hebrews, perhaps more than any other New Testament book, reminds us clearly it was the Old Testament which served as Scripture for the first generation church and Christians. In fact, Hebrews appears to be a sermon, of sorts, based upon the Old Testament and a particular method of interpretation which makes it difficult to follow at best. This is particularly evident in the text before us.

One thing, however, seems clear. It appears to have been written to Christians who needed to be warned and provoked concerning the seriousness of their fatigue and listlessness with regard to the faith. Although the temptations and persecutions faced by these first century Christians we call "the Hebrews" were, no doubt, different from our own, our author's message remains appropriate and relevant for every generation of Christians which struggles with "drooping hands" and "weak knees" (12:12).

The writer of Hebrews is concerned for the spiritual health of his audience. His desire is to bring them to a confident faith which will produce a lasting hope and a proper and acceptable worship. His example and his desire would be a worthy goal for ministers and church leaders of each generation. Here, there is a word of God for us, too!

What we know about the spiritual condition of "the Hebrews" must be deduced from the exhortations which our author gives them. But how about Christians who read this message today? How would *you* describe the condition of the church today? What is the status of our spiritual health as individual Christians, as a denomination, and as the Christian Church in general? As a Baptist minister and a student of the Bible these questions alarm me. Perhaps the questions are not so bad, but honest answers to them, I am afraid, would be a reproach to many of us. Would there be better words than these to describe the condition of many Southern Baptists just now: "drooping hands" and "weak knees"? We are listless to the point of lethargy.

The Christians who received the message of the book of Hebrews faced persecution, situations so severe that the possibility arose that some might even give up their faith. Baptists in the United States today face little, if any, of what may be called persecution. Christians are not persecuted; more likely they are ignored. What is there about us that is worthy of persecution? We are too busy fighting among ourselves over matters about which God could not care less while the world rushes on its way apart from his Christ. It is life patterned on the life of Christ which makes the world sit up and take notice of Christians, not fighting over fine points of doctrine. Fighting about the worship of a book prevents us from the proper worship of God "with reverence and awe" (12:28), which then enables us to "see to it that no one fail to obtain the grace of God" (12:15).

So the author of Hebrews reminds his audience, and he would remind us also, to find strength and power for hands held high and body erect. Let the path be smoothed and every obstacle removed over which the lame Christian and church may trip and fall (12:13). Here is a word of God for us!

Perhaps there was a spirit of disagreement among these Christians to whom our text is addressed. But it could not be more serious than that which exists today. There must be no strife or dissension among us because, as the author clearly points out, such prevents Christians from the holiness without which "no one may see the Lord" (12:14; cf. Ex. 33:20-23). Here, as in verses 18 and following, the author calls upon the language of the presence of God. He desires to call his audience to a faith which has the power to become directly aware of

God's presence. It is impossible for us to enter the presence of God for "acceptable worship" (12:28) when we are spiritually contaminated by dissension and a "root of bitterness" which has sprung up in our midst. We must seek the highway, the straight paths of integrity, and shun the temptation to irrelevance.

How can our major concerns center around denominational control and doctrinal conformity when there are countless thousands who will die this day simply because of the lack of the nutrients of life? How can we have as our major concern the enforcement the use of certain emotional code-words, when our small planet races on toward self-destruction because militarism is chosen and trusted rather than Christ's way of peace? With no integrity whatsoever we devote our energies to bickering, back-biting and name-calling, while a lost humanity looks upon a church that is powerless to change the ills which beset the world.

We must be especially watchful and keep anxious guard over the flock of our churches, making sure that we each live up to our Christian vocation, lest a single unworthy member rise up like a poisonous weed to defile everything about us (12:15). Will Southern Baptists be as careless as Esau and sell our spiritual birthright of religious liberty, local church autonomy, priesthood of believers and cooperating in missions, for a narrow-minded, anti-intellectual doctrinal conformity? The author of Hebrews reminded his audience of the serious consequences of spiritual suicide. Later Esau sought the blessing of his father, but found rejection instead and no opportunity for repentance. What price will Southern Baptists pay for the sin of missed opportunity if we throw away our witness in the world for a mess of meaningless and irrelevant rhetoric? Disobedience brings its awful penalty. God's work and witness in the world is not limited to Southern Baptists. If we will not be his God-reverencing, prophetic people, he will raise up another. The plan for the ages will not be thwarted by our narrowness of mind and lip-service to his Word which we otherwise ignore.

We have been weakened as a denomination because our energies have been misdirected away from missions and ministry which flow naturally from "proper worship." Our witness in the world has suffered as a result of actions and words which reveal individuals with less than pure motives and a less than adequate understanding of integrity with regard to the Christian faith. Thus with the author of Hebrews we must call for nothing less than lifted hands, strengthened knees, and smooth paths lest one more stumble lead to our complete dislocation. Our aim must be "peace with all" and "holiness" without which we may not see God.

Perhaps this is the heart of the matter. Our eyes are not upon God. Our author recalls to our memory the events of Sinai where God's presence and law were revealed to the people. Yahweh's theophany at Sinai was complete with "fire," "thick darkness," "deep gloom," "storm," and "the sound of the trumpet" (12:18-19; cf. Ex. 19:12-21; Deut. 4:11-12; 5:22-27). These words were a part of the Israel's vocabulary for communicating the nearness of God's presence. The response of Moses and the people to this experience was "trembling with fear." (12:21). This is the proper Old Testament response when God's presence is experienced. When humans encounter the presence of God they are set in their place and see themselves for what they are — sinners. All pride of knowledge, all spiritual arrogance, all self-deception goes by the board. An encounter with God brings about a proper understanding of ourselves and our lack of "holiness" before a holy God.

But the image does not stop there for the writer of Hebrews. The encounter of Moses and the people at Sinai is but an earthly foretaste of an even greater reality in the light of Jesus Christ. In times gone by God spoke from Sinai, the earthly mountain, and made covenant with his people. Now God speaks through Jesus, "the mediator of a new covenant" whose blood does not call out for vengeance, like that of Abel (Gen. 4:10), but calls out graciously for love and mercy (12:22-24).

"See that you do not refuse him who is speaking . . . much less shall we escape if we reject him who warns from heaven" (12:25). Again our author reminds us that how we respond when God speaks is a serious matter. Disobedience is quite serious! We must ask ourselves if, indeed, our eyes and ears are attuned to Jesus Christ through whom God had spoken clearly and decisively. What does it cost to refuse him? Baptists must hear a word from God in this exhortation of the writer to the Hebrews. God's voice "shook the earth" when he spoke from Sinai, but the promise has been given that a final "shaking" is yet to come. What responsibility is ours to live and communicate the love of God in Christ in our world just now!

What God has spoken through Jesus Christ is his word for us and his desire for our lives, both individually and corporately. It is a word which should stir even the most complacent hearts and minds in Christ's church. It is a word which, when heard, will help us focus our eyes gratefully upon "a kingdom that cannot be shaken." Jesus was never concerned to take over the religious establishment of his day in order to impose doctrinal conformity. He was concerned to bring God's gracious word of love and forgiveness and healing to those who were hurt, needful, and in pain, to those who were sinners. The religious orthodox, the punctilious Pharisees, could not understand or accept the servant model chosen by our Lord.

Our author's concern is spiritual health and proper worship. "Let us offer to God acceptable worship, with reverence and awe" (12:28). Again, perhaps the root of our problems is that we do not offer acceptable worship. We do not really encounter the presence of God in the sense that the Bible suggests is possible.

Statistics reveal that on any given Sunday less than half of the 14 million Southern Baptists join their congregational assembly for worship. And how many of those who go do anything to prepare for worship? Once they arrive, how often do they find an order of service, a song, a sermon which has been carefully planned to bring the congregation to an awareness of the presence of God? Worship, which is vitally important for the life of Christians, is ignored! We have "preaching" or "evangelistic" services rather than "worship" services. We meet in auditoriums rather than sanctuaries. We desire entertainment and television spectaculars rather than meaningful worship with "reverence and awe."

The author of Hebrews knew well that spiritual health and acceptable worship go hand in hand. Is there not a word of

God for contemporary Christians in this exhortation? Is there not a message for Southern Baptists here? The author of Hebrews concludes his appeal with a reference to Deuteronomy 4:24 (cf. Deut. 9:3; 2 Thess. 1:7-8), "for our God is a consuming fire." Our author does much to challenge our simple conception of God as an easy-going old grandfather. His is the proper Old Testament conception of God as one who takes relationship seriously. The God who is a "devouring fire" is a "jealous God" (Deut. 4:24). The Old Testament describes a God who is jealous of his relationship with his covenant people. How much more so the God who shows his love for us in one like Jesus! How jealous are we of our relationship to him? How jealous are we to protect our witness? How jealous are we to guard our worship lest it be anything less than proper?

Proper worship with reverence and awe will bring us spiritual health and a confident faith. Let hands be given strength to be held up straight! Let knees be supplied with the power to sustain the body erect! Let a spirit of peace be cultivated in our midst! May we strive to be consecrated and obtain a faith which will lead us into the very presence of God! May his presence empower us to live his love in our world and make that love contagious!

18

A Conspiracy for Life

Hebrews 13:1-6

James M. Pitts
Chaplain, Furman University, Greenville, Sorth Carolina

Thanks to industrial growth, affluence and an insatiable appetite for more and more, ecologists warn of cosmic halitosis. The world, they say, is suffering from bad breath! Some laugh away the smoke and fumes and poisonous vapor that choke the common breath of all. They smile and say, "Bad breath is better than no breath at all." After all, how do you pour Listerine down a whole planet's throat?

To breathe, to breathe together is the rhythm and basis for life and community. Breathing together or choking separately is not only a global concern. In my opinion, it is a personal concern for each of us who inhabit this community. My concern is more than air and water, it focuses on the quality of life we live in relationship to one another.

No amount of suburban landscaping or urban renewal can hide the thin line which separates civilization and the jungle. That line is crossed whenever we stop caring. That thin line is crossed when we close our eyes to the process of separation and dehumanization, with its various acts of violence and aggression.

Life in community, especially within the family of faith, is a matter of breathing, just like it is in the physical environment. Either we breathe together or we choke separately. "To conspire" is to breathe together. To conspire to agree in thought, to unite and combine for a purpose and effect. The alternative is to expire, which means to give up the breath of life, to die.

Addressing some Christians who were in danger of passing away, the writer of Hebrews encouraged them to make an attitude adjustment. Carefully he reviews for them the imperatives of the Christian faith. The foundational requirements for life together, he suggests, include brotherly love, hospitality to strangers, care for prisoners, purity in marriage, and freedom from concern about money.

Initially, his simple suggestions may sound superficial. After careful consideration, they are revolutionary. Taken seriously, they will produce a radical revision in our understanding of life together as Christians. As the writer proceeds, we realize there is an increasing difficulty in these demands.

First he admonishes, "Let brotherly love continue." The focus is not just on a warm glow, but committed care for the physical and material needs of others. This love is not emotional, hysterical spasms and nostalgic religious sentimentality. This is a tough and realistic love that cares in a practical and supportive manner. We must not pretend that we don't need one another. Each and every one is important and necessary to our fellowship. Christians do not thrive in isolation. As a community, our faith is fed and formed by involvement with our brothers and sisters. Interaction offers comfort and challenge.

The early Christians understood their responsibility to love one another. Any member who had possessions and saw his brother or sister in need and then did nothing in response, abandoned his ability to claim the love of God dwelling in his heart.

The first admonition in this conspiracy for life, love for the immediate community members, was followed by love for strangers. The love of the Christian went beyond the congregational walls. It crossed the boundary from those who were settled and familiar to those who were itinerant and unknown. Generally, we love people in our own community. To move outside toward strangers challenges our selfishness and self-imposed provincial limits of accountability.

Henri Nouwen properly suggests that "hospitality" is the primary task of Christian ministry. Hospitality offers tired and exhausted travelers a place of relaxation and peace, friendship to the lonely wanderer, food and drink to the hungry and thirsty. Hospitality provides a warm welcome with appropriate attention, acceptance without unnecessary questions and encouragement for the on-going journey.

In our day, we have assumed that hospitality is the responsibility of the commercial restauranteur and hotel manager. The tradition of non-commercial hospitality, especially in less affluent times, was not only needful, but the expected norm. When strangers came, the Christian community expected to entertain and assist them in finding food, clean clothing and lodging. To neglect a stranger was to inflict hardship and suffering.

The custom of hospitality to the sojourner was an integral part of mid-eastern culture. Whether the host was rich or poor, he viewed the unanticipated guest not as an imposition but as an honored opportunity. Especially for the Bedouin, the nomadic Arab of the desert, the availability of hospitality in his harsh, waterless, over-exposed, sand strewn environment may mark the difference between life and death. In that sun glare world, you do not long survive alone. A supportive network of friends and acquaintances is necessary if life is going to have quality and community. Our interdependence for life's essentials is equally true in town settings, even though we may not see the servants that provide us clear water, electricity and other necessities for human habitation.

Not only were Christians fulfilling their religious responsibility by showing hospitality to strangers, some even entertained angels without knowing it. On occasions the stranger turned out to be a messenger of God. Inviting a stranger who had walked with them from Jerusalem to Emmaus to come in and be their guest at dinner became a surprise encounter between the risen Christ and two of his discouraged followers.

In our city, for several generations there has been a small group of Christians who take this counsel literally concerning offering hospitality to strangers. The director of the local rescue mission states that "if a man does not have a friend anywhere else, he has one here." Nightly, his center feeds and houses more than a hundred transients. Homeless men, women and children are offered a clean and safe place to sleep, nourishing food, spirited inspiration and practical guidance for coping with their particular crisis. As a person who takes the Scripture seriously, he is following the Lord's mandate, knowing that "inasmuch as you did it for the least of these, my brethren, you did it for me."

Not stopping with brotherly love and hospitality to strangers, the writer of Hebrews now suggests an additional group. They are even more challenging than known colleagues and strangers off the street. He wants us to identify with those in prison. Now for straight, self-righteous folks that is a little too much, don't you think? Many Christians today take pride in being law-abiding citizens. They have never been in jail, not even to visit. They forget that some of the biblical persons whose names we honor were locked up. This is true of others in our spiritual ancestry, especially dissenters in the free church tradition.

We quickly forget that the early Christian faithful were frequently thrown into prison because of their position in the fellowship and activities of witness. When persons are being persecuted, suffering and dying for their faith, there is a tendency to withdraw or deny any association with them in order to avoid a similar fate. The apostle Peter certainly did just that when Jesus was in jail on the night his Lord was arrested.

Expressing identity with prisoners by visiting and bringing food and other necessities may be interpreted as sympathy and shared political and religious views. Especially for Christians undergoing persecution, this identification is important, not only as an expression of brotherly love, but also for their very survival. This identification should go beyond those imprisoned to include those who are ill-treated, since they, too, are a part of the body of believers. The Christian fellowship is to search out the abused, the mistreated, and the victims of injustice and aggression.

A bold identification with the victims of suffering and neglect is seen in the work of Mother Teresa of Calcutta. With her Missionaries of Charity, she searches out the dying, poor and abandoned elderly and infants. To the defenseless and vulnerable members of humanity, she offers comfort and nurture. Her hospices and homes are expressions of incarnate love. Through their work with the poor and broken bodies of these throw-aways of society, they minister as they would with Jesus and for Jesus and to Jesus.

Henry Parr, a young attorney and alumnus of Furman, became interested in the work of Mother Teresa. Moved by this ministry of compassionate care, he committed himself to go to India as a volunteer. Upon returning home, Henry was invited to present a slide show and give a talk on his experience. This presentation was very moving, but not from oratorical eloquence or emotional enthusiasm.

The fan of the slide projector and the clicking of its mechanism formed the background music of Henry's softly stated commentary. The scenes of squalor, the staring eyes, drawn and emaciated bodies of people who had been left on the street to die, who are now being cared for in sparse but clean houses of mercy, were overwhelmingly powerful. It was as if each slide was invisibly sub-titled "Inasmuch as you do it unto the least of these, my brethren . . . "

With the projector off and the lights in the small auditorium on, we had a time for conversation. An attractive, well groomed and stylishly dressed sophomore young woman inquired, "Does Mother Teresa ever give a Christian witness?" The response to her question tried to help her understand that her life of poverty, caring action, kind words, and reverent silences were a Christian witness. The young lady obviously was not satisfied with that answer. She went on to inquire, "Why was Mother Teresa not handing out printed Scripture portions and preaching on street corners?" How can anyone be doing the Lord's work who is not appearing on a cable television talk show, running a promotional blitz with a toll-free response line, giving concerts and publishing books? Seduced by our contemporary culture's religious enthusiasm, the simple life of quiet and sacrificial service was both inadequate and alien to that young woman. She was not aware that if anyone suffers within the body of Christ, all are pained. To respond to that hurt is ministry with Christ and for Christ and even to Christ.

The recommendations for interdependent living within the bounds of Christian community continue with an affirmation of marriage. This is the only mention of marriage in

Hebrews. The marital relationship is to be honored in every respect. The marriage bed is to be undefiled. Faithfulness is in; adultery and fornication are out. Within the family of faith, the stress is on purity in the marital relationship. The prohibition is not against sexuality, but against promiscuity.

As if he were saving the most controversial for the last, the writer then moves on to one's attitude toward money. This is another contrast between the way of life recommended within the Christian family as compared to the attitudes and life styles of the uncommitted and unaffiliated. The Christians are encouraged to put greed out of their lives and to be content with whatever they had. Perhaps there was a restlessness within the Christian community about giving all. The counsel was to be courageous and give up anxiety about money and other material things. They are to trust in the Lord, who is their helper. They were to choose poverty voluntarily and to be confident in God's care.

These were not the first nor the last believers to hear that the gospel way encourages a new relationship to material possessions. Some 800 years ago, a man was born who enthusiastically embraced poverty. His name was Francis, Francis of Assisi. He passionately rejected wealth, affluence, property and material goods. These were seen by Francis as deterrents to Christian community and union with God. Francis saw in his own life how concern for things material had separated him from his own father. He saw how obsession with money could turn one's vision from the needs of others to the fulfillment of self-interest. He looked at the church of his day, with its vast wealth and endowments, its houses and servants, and called the church to return to the Saviour who had no place to lay his head.

By personal choice, Francis became the Little Poor Man of God's Downward Way. He warned his followers not to accept pay for their work, believing that the fewer one's possessions, the freer one was to serve God. "If we possess property," he said, "we should need arms to defend it. Property is the source of quarrels and lawsuits, and is an obstacle to the love of God and one's neighbor."

The freely chosen poverty of Francis was a way to God; the socially imposed poverty of many is a way to despair and alienation. Like Jesus, Francis realized that God's call takes us beyond materialism to a joyful, peaceful, loving and simple life.

Somewhere deep in our hearts we already know that success, fame, influence, power and money do not give us the inner joy and peace for which we long. Somewhere we can even sense a certain envy of those who have shed all their worldly ambitions and live their lives in simple obedience toward God.

The good news of God announces a unique and transforming moment in human affairs. God was in Christ, redeeming and reconciling the world to himself. God became flesh and dwelt among us in the person of Jesus.

That event calls for a new way of living by those whose lives have been apprehended by that divine-human reality. There is to be a difference in the attitudes and life styles of believers. No longer living detached, self-absorbed, isolated lives, the followers of Christ are together in a caring, loving, supportive and nurturing community. Love for brothers and sisters, hospitality to strangers, identification with prisoners and the mistreated, faithfulness in marriage and unconcern for money are a part of the Christian conspiracy for life. The Scripture clearly commends these attitudes and activities for those who are committed to Christ and his way.

19

The Great Shepherd of the Sheep

Hebrews 13:20-21

James M. Pitts
Chaplain, Furman University, Greenville, Sorth Carolina

From the opening to the close of Scripture, encompassing both Old and New Testaments, a common biblical metaphor is that of shepherds and sheep. However, it is a surprise when the writer of the Letter to the Hebrews selects a shepherd-sheep analogy in his benediction. This concluding prayer is his initial and only use of this pastoral figure. Expecting to hear of "our great high priest", he speaks instead of "the great shepherd of the sheep". In choosing this liturgical refrain, he echoes a popular biblical theme. Shepherd and sheep references occur hundreds of times.

In the Genesis story, Abel, the sheep keeper, was murdered by his brother, Cain, the farmer. This tragedy followed Abel's sacrificial offering of the first of his flock. Cain, believing his agricultural gift was not preferred by God, killed his brother in a jealous rage. In the dawn of human story, a shepherd's blood was spilled on the ground.

At the conclusion of salvation-history, the shepherd-sheep motif speaks of the Lamb, slain from the foundation of the world, who now occupies the throne of God.

Sheep and shepherds were an integral part of daily life in the ancient biblical world. Central to the Palestinian economy and life style of pastoral people, sheep provided food to eat, milk to drink, wool for weaving, covering for tents, a medium of exchange and a source of sacrifice for offerings.

The shepherd was a common figure in mid-east culture. In biblical times, he was more prevalent than Ronald McDonald,

Santa Claus, or the Easter Bunny in today's suburbia. An everyday personage in yesteryear, shepherds literally were on every vegetated hill and in every green valley. Shepherds, with flowing head coverings and graceful robes, walking ahead of the sheep and sometimes carrying lambs in their arms, were a normal part of the working scene.

Like most suburban or city residents, I had never met a real shepherd or come into contact with sheep. My knowledge was those animals pictured in Sunday School literature, or cute television cartoon characters, like ventriloquist Sherri Lewis' "Lamb-chop." Even my home church in its affluent sophistication, did not have folks grow beards and wear bath robes to stage a Christmas or Easter tableau.

Being so culturally deprived, you can imagine my surprise this spring in Israel when I saw a real, honest to goodness, shepherd. My host, Khalil Janho, a Furman alumnus of 1976, promising me a non-tourist tour, took me for a ride in and around Judea. Travelling the narrow, winding roads east of Bethlehem, our car came over the crest of the hill and to a sudden stop. Before us a shepherd and his flock were crossing the road. Camera in hand, I jumped out of the car to capture that "shepherd with his sheep" scene on film. Oblivious to my presence, either burned out on tourists toting cameras, or simply too busy to bother to pose, the shepherd led his sheep on toward their next grazing site. With staff in hand, his eyes on the sheep and the trail ahead, the shepherd's face turned toward his pastoral task and purposely away from my intrusion into his life and work.

Frustrated that such a picturesque moment was lost, I then laughed at myself for assuming that it was a shepherd's responsibility to pause and pose. He was not an Indian chief, outside a Cherokee reservation store, demeaned to stand and smile the day long for tourist Polaroids. That shepherd was the real thing.

He was no romantic figure, just an ordinary working man with responsibility to find food for his flock and to protect them from harm. Without a shepherd, the sheep will starve or fall as easy prey. With the shepherd's care and supervision, the sheep are secure.

Separated by years and miles, we need to be reminded that shepherding in the climatic conditions of Palestine was a demanding and sometimes a hazardous occupation. During the long dry season, it was necessary to move the flocks considerable distances in search of good pastures; suitable resting and watering places had to be found; robbers and wild beasts occasionally hid in the shadows of valleys. The shepherd was with his flock day and night, often in remote places far from home. He had to be skilled in keeping his flock together, in finding wanderers and stragglers, in recognizing the ailments of his sheep and knowing how to cure them, and in ensuring the safety of the vulnerable members of the flock. His unsettled, dangerous, semi-nomadic life makes him a slightly ambiguous figure — perhaps like the cowboy of the "Wild West." There is a mixture of tenderness and toughness in the character of the shepherd.

In rabbinic writings, shepherds were viewed with suspicion and in a negative way. Shepherds and Bedouins were accused of handling stolen goods and trespassing on other people's pastureland. Shepherds, seen in common with publicans and tax gatherers, were not permitted to hold judicial office or give evidence in court. Perhaps this was an expression of the age-old tension between the sojourner and the settled, the desert sand and the village of the sown. The nomadic life has always been viewed with hostility by the agriculturally stable.

The sheep and shepherd relationship is dramatically and positively used by writers, poets and prophets of the Old Testament. The 23rd Psalm, the classic text learned by heart, recited in concert from memory, affirms:

"The Lord is my shepherd, I shall not want." The shepherd's concern for the unity of his flock is revealed by Ezekiel:

> I will look for those who are lost, bring back those that wander off, bandage those that are hurt, and heal those that are sick. (34:16).

> They shall all have one shepherd . . . they shall dwell in the land where your fathers dwelt . . . I will make a covenant of peace with them . . . and I will bless them (37:24-26).

Jeremiah, speaking on behalf of God concerning the shepherds who care for his people, promised:

> I will gather the remnant of my flock out of all the countries where I have driven them, and I will bring them back to their fold, and they shall be fruitful and multiply. I will set shepherds over them who will care for them, and they shall fear no more, nor be dismayed, neither shall any be missing, says the Lord (23:3,4).

In second Isaiah, the writer announces:

> Behold, the Lord comes with might and his arm rules for him; behold, his reward is with him, and his recompense before him. He will feed his flock like a shepherd, he will gather the lambs in his arms, he will carry them in his bosom, and gently lead those that are with young (40:10,11).

In Luke's nativity story, it is shepherds who were called to witness the Messiah's birth. They were sent by angels to an animal stall, whose location they clearly knew, perhaps because they had used the space for their own flocks. The choice of shepherds, that rough and questionable group, as first witnesses of Jesus' birth harmonizes with Luke's stress on the humanity of the nativity.

> He has brought down mighty kings from their thrones, and lifted up the lowly (1:52).

With this figurative-theological language tradition of the shepherd and the sheep, it is no surprise when the New Testament makes the application to Jesus and his followers.

Mark's Gospel describes the Lord's concern for humanity, when upon seeing a crowd, Jesus "had compassion on them, because they were like sheep without a shepherd, and he began to teach them many things" (6:34).

In his teaching, Jesus uses the shepherd image to express God's strenuous and constant concern for those who have gone astray. Jesus appropriates the shepherd metaphor to interpret himself: "I am the good shepherd" (John 10:11).

Christ is the shepherd, who saves and sustains the life of all who come under his pastoral care. "I am the door of the sheep . . . if anyone enters by me, he will be saved, and will go in and out and find pasture" (John 10:7-9).

The surprise, the twist of the metaphor, unprecedented and unexpected, is when the Son of God, the Good Shepherd, announces his intention to die.

Biblical faith can conceive of Israel or the Servant of God dying on behalf of God's cause in the world, but not of God himself dying. Unheard of! The prophets never spoke of God as Shepherd dying for the sheep. Jesus takes the metaphor further:

> I am the good shepherd. The good shepherd lays down his life for the sheep . . . so there shall be one flock, one shepherd.
>
> For this reason the Father loves me, because I lay down my life, that I may take it again. No one takes it from me, but I lay it down on my own accord, and I have power to take it again. This charge I have received from my Father (John 10:11,16c-18).

The surprise, the shock, is that the shepherd so identifies himself with his flock that he takes the place of the sacrificial lamb. The ultimate act of love is to die a sacrificial death. The good shepherd becomes the sacrificial lamb. The shepherd's staff becomes the cross of the Lamb of God.

In the tradition of the good shepherds who went before, such as Abraham, Moses, and David, the greatest shepherd of all, Jesus, "the trail blazer" to salvation, leads the way out of the captivity of sin, through the wilderness of death, to the promised land of life eternal.

The good and great shepherd's purpose was accurately assessed by John the Baptist, when he saw Jesus coming for baptism in the Jordan. He announced then and for now, "Behold the Lamb of God, who takes away the sin of the world" (John 1:29).

The writer of Hebrews offers this benediction:

> Now may the God of peace who brought again from the dead our Lord Jesus, the great shepherd of the sheep, by the blood of the

> eternal covenant, equip you with everything good that you may do his will, working in you that which is pleasing in his sight, through Jesus Christ; to whom be glory for ever and ever. Amen (13:20,21).

Through the leadership of Christ, the good and great shepherd, who is also the Lamb of God, may such peace and blessing, encouragement and purpose, be yours.

Thorwald Lorenzen, professor of systematic theology and ethics, International Baptist Theological Seminary, Ruschlikon, Switzerland. An alumnus of the Ruschlikon Seminary, he earned the Doctor of Theology degree from the University of Zurich.

C. David Matthews, senior minister, First Baptist Church, Greenville, South Carolina. Dr. Matthews is a graduate of Baylor University and Southwestern Baptist Theological Seminary, Fort Worth, Texas. Prior to his present position, he was pastor of the Seventh & James Baptist Church, Waco, Texas. In 1984 he gave the E. Y. Mullins Lectures on preaching at Southern Seminary.

Edgar V. McKnight, the William R. Kenan, Jr. Professor of Religion, Furman University, Greenville, South Carolina. A graduate of the College of Charleston, The Southern Baptist Theological Seminary, and Oxford University, author of several texts and numerous scholarly articles, he is past president of The National Association of Baptist Professors of Religion, and the Society of Biblical Literature/Southeast.

Dale Moody was the Joseph Emerson Brown Professor of Christian Theology, The Southern Baptist Theological Seminary, Louisville, Kentucky before his retirement. A graduate of Baylor University, Southern Seminary and Oxford University, he also taught at the University of Heidelberg, Germany and the Gregorian University, Rome, Italy. Author of numerous articles and books, his most recent publication is *The Word of Truth.*

Robert C. Mulkey, minister, First Baptist Church, DeLand, Florida. This graduate of Furman University and The Southern Baptist Theological Seminary served congregations in Kentucky and South Carolina prior to his present pastorate.

James M. Pitts, chaplain, Furman University, Greenville, South Carolina. He is a graduate of Furman University, Southeastern Baptist Theological Seminary and The Southern Baptist Theological Seminary. Prior to his present position he was a pastor in Virginia, Alabama and South Carolina.

T. C. Smith, professor of religion emeritus, Furman University, Greenville, South Carolina. He is a graduate of Louisiana College, Pineville, Louisiana, The Southern Baptist Theological Seminary and the University of Edinburgh, Scotland. Author of *The Broadman Bible Commentary on Acts*, he recently has served as a visiting professor at both Southern and Southeastern Seminaries.

Richard Spencer, professor of New Testament, Southeastern Baptist Theological Seminary. A graduate of Mars Hill College, Southeastern Seminary and Emory University, Atlanta, Georgia, Dr. Spencer was a pastor in North Carolina and an instructor at Candler School of Theology before joining the faculty at Southeastern.

Frank Stagg, senior professor of New Testament Studies, The Southern Baptist Theological Seminary, Louisville, Kentucky. A graduate of Louisiana College, Pineville, Louisiana and The Southern Baptist Seminary, his publications include *The Broadman Bible Commentary* volumes on *Matthew* and *Philippians*, and most recently, *The Bible Speaks on Aging*.

Cecil P. Staton, Jr., graduate student at Regent's Park College, University of Oxford, Oxford, England. An alumnus of Furman University and Southeastern Baptist Theological Seminary, The Reverend Mr. Staton has served churches in both North and South Carolina.

John Sullivan, minister, Broadmoor Baptist Church, Shreveport, Louisiana. An alumnus of Grand Canyon Baptist College and Southwestern Baptist Theological Seminary, Dr. Sullivan has also pastored in Arizona and Texas.